RUN YOUR OWN RACE

12 Steps to Building Your Powerful Personal Brand

Sidney Evans, MBA

Printed in the United States of America
2018 First Edition
10 9 8 7 6 5 4 3 2 1

Subject Index:
Evans, Sidney
Title: Run Your Own Race: 12 Steps to Building Your Powerful Personal Brand
1. Brand Strategy 2. Branding 3. Leadership 4. Business 5. Technology 6. Social Media 7. Marketing

Library of Congress Card Catalog Number:
Paperback ISBN: 978-0-578-51019-4

www.sidneyevans.com

PRAISES...
THE RACE IS YOURS TO WIN

"The 21st century, replete with global intricacies, is a clear testament to the fact that Darwin was right. To survive, organizations and individuals must provide unique services and products to a highly complex, global marketplace. The pathway to extinction looms ahead when such distinctiveness is not achieved.

Sidney Evans, the author of *Run Your Own Race*, understands such principals well. His pragmatic, insightful manual presents a workable one-year plan to help individuals shape their *own* distinctive brand. Using the acronym, RACE (*Reflect, Actualize, Commit, Evolve*), Evans incorporates fundamental assessment questions (*"what three words best describe you?"*), personal anecdotes, and inspirational quotes to highlight the strategic skillsets necessary to "stand out" effectively. Evans adeptly illustrates with the metaphoric marathon race, that personal brands are not determined overnight but rather are dependent on focus, preparation, and accurate self-assessment. The book is written in such a way that the reader is able to "pace" him or herself through the various branding phases over a realistic (one-year) period of time.

Run Your Own Race should, in fact, be required reading for all individuals prior to embarking on an initial career path or those considering a career change. It is a down-to-earth, uplifting book filled with practical advice for fine-tuning one's personal reputation and brand."

- Linda L. Neider, Ph.D., Professor of Management, University of Miami, and Co-Author, the Authentic Leadership Inventory

"Sidney is one of our most prominent contributors at *Branding Mag*, whom we have all come to call a *talent wrangler*. He is an authentic, personable, conversationalist, that has the ability to exude a unique identity that is informed, yet independent. In essence, there is no winning in branding: You may watch what others do, gather pros and cons, but those who take the time to focus on quality (rather than quantity) will be the ones to run forever. Sidney has been running his race, conscientious of the driving force that is branding, for quite some time now and has many versatile experiences to show for it. He embodies the notion that branding, while something necessary, is something to be taken with stride. He embodies a distinctness reminiscent of "to each his own.""

- Flavia Barbat
Editor-in-Chief
Brandingmag
www.brandingmag.com

"Personal Development, Growth, and Branding is a continuous evolutionary need of humankind as we move ever further into the Information Age. *Run Your Own Race* is a refreshing reminder that we all need to get back to the basics. As I have read quite often, any plan without action is merely a dream. Planning to do planning will result in no tangible achievements for anyone. Sidney has blessed us all with a comprehensive plan to take back ownership of self. Self-care is not being selfish about sharing your value with society, it actually means sharing your best version of you with the world. By being introspective first to develop our best version of self, we are able to provide the world with our best, most salient talents. "The 12 Steps to Building Your Personal Brand" provides a roadmap to achieving our redefined and recalibrated optimal self. The pace is everything in life. We need to enjoy the journey just as much as the destination. *Run Your Own Race* allows us to succinctly create better habits and document a plan of action to achieve our own goals."

- Johnny "Rio" Fultz,
CEO of RIO[3] Consulting

"Since I work on brands all day long it is refreshing to find a book that will help me to better serve clients and mentees who are interested in developing their personal brand. In *Run Your Own Race*, Syd Evans presents a straight-forward, simple and workable guide to standing out in your field, no matter how cluttered it might be. A must-read if you are looking to advance your career and be recognized as a voice to be heard."

Run Your Own Race cuts through a whole lot of noise and presents a field guide to creating a strong personal brand. I recommend it to anyone who really cares about advancing their career and rising to the top of their game."
- Omar A. Hikal
CEO, The Brand Company
Cairo, Egypt

"Syd Evans will redefine and chart a fresh course in the field of brand marketing. His new book, *Run Your Own Race*, places the golden key in the hands of everyone desiring to brand or rebrand themselves in The New Media Age. Specifically, the book helps one understand not to ignore their calling to be great; and to realize that hearing and understanding the oft-ignored voice inside of you is the foundation for personal branding success. But it does not end there, likening the journey of self-branding to a race, Evans is less concerned with when you finish your journey but encouraging his readers to be fully equipped, well informed and to savor every step of the process."
- Michael L. Clark
VP Advertising Sales, TheGrio

"Upwardly professionals and entrepreneurs, eagerly desiring success, often bypass the importance of building their own personal brands. *Run Your Own Race* is an accessible, action-oriented motivational book, providing long-held expertise,

currently actualized by global visionaries. Utilize the wisdom detailed in *Run Your Own Race* to jumpstart your life and your business!"
- Sabrina Lamb
Founding CEO

"Anyone on the journey of developing a personal brand will want to read this book! Sidney Evans' has managed to create a valuable reference and "training manual", packed with personal branding insights and actions. This book will be a resource for years to come, as readers embark upon their marathon of developing an influential personal brand."
- Donovan Fowke,
CEO of Symbicore Inc.

Foreword
Run Your Own Race

Steve Olenski

In one of the opening sections of his book, Sidney has what he refers to as **THE WARM-UP.** The section begins with a quote you're probably familiar with: *"Most people can tell you what they do, but very few can tell you why they do it."*

Well, I want to tell you the WHY as it relates to my writing the Foreword for this book because, well the answer is easy: because Sidney asked me. It really was and is that simple. It took me all of 3 seconds to say yes. I would do anything for him.

Sidney has that kind of effect on people. It's a gift and it's quite rare. And his effect and impact, at least on me, was instantaneous. I first met Sidney in Miami at the 2017 Major League Baseball All-Star Game. I was in town doing a piece for *Forbes* on Mastercard, one of the major brand sponsors of the game.

To say we hit it off immediately would be a massive understatement. We both knew we were destined to become 'brothers' and that's even *before* we knew had a Philly connection. I could literally feel his passion coming from his words as we spoke that day. We talked about many subjects but branding and personal branding was chief among them.

Fast-forward to today and it is a natural evolution for someone such as Sidney – who is the living embodiment of personal branding and what it can do for you not only professionally but spiritually, emotionally and mentally – to share his innermost thoughts, ideas and advice.

I won't tell you to enjoy the book because I already know you will. But do yourself a favor and get to know Sidney. You can thank me later.

Acknowledgements

The process of writing my first book has been humbling and much more difficult than I could ever imagine yet equally as fulfilling. This book would not be possible without my the love, sacrifice and unwavering support of my Grandparents, Kelsie & Irene, my parents, Robin & Sidney and my tribe. Their immeasurable level of sacrifice coupled as well as believe in my purpose has been transformative.

To my tribe, thank you...thank you for always believing in me and encouraging me to live my passion. I can not thank you enough. You have encouraged me, pushed me and held me accountable. For that, I am eternally grateful! The true definition of friendship is when you want your to break new ground!

To my endorsers and mentors, I can't thank you enough for your kind words and support throughout this process.

Special thanks to Steve Olenski, CMO Whisperer! Brothers for LIFE!

Please be very clear, WE ALL WIN together!

TABLE OF CONTENTS

Reflect
Actualize
Commit
Evolve

R= REFLECT

Each time I see the Upside-Down Man
Standing in the water,
I look at him and start to laugh, ...
For maybe in another world
Another time
Another town,
Maybe HE is right side up
And I am upside down.
    - Shel Silverstein

THE WARM-UP

> *"Most people can tell you what they do, but very few can tell you why they do it."*

Pace yourself. Building your powerful personal brand is not for sprinters. It requires a well-planned strategy and commitment to a routine that gradually moves you closer to your passion and purpose. If your goal is to quit your job next week and instantly become rich and famous, then this is not the tool for you.

What is personal branding? Personal branding is an individual commitment to perform intentional tasks to market yourself and career as a bonafide brand, similar to recognizable corporate brands. Every unique characteristic and skillset that you have is what differentiates your personal brand from others. I believe that your personal brand is your insatiable *Why*. Think about *why* you do what you do. What motivates you? What tasks make you feel fulfilled? Are you striving to become better? Personal branding embarks upon the activities that you need to carry out each day by delivering your core values to your desired target audience. Regardless of where you are in your career, personal branding is a vital skill set. It encompasses presenting your true authentic self to the world at *all* times.

So often I meet people in various business and social settings and later research them online to get a fuller picture of who they are. I can't tell you how shocked I am when I try to piece together the personalities of the individual I just met in person and the individual in the photos and online fingerprint. Which one is the impersonator? The two people are not even close in appearance, demeanor or values. Who are you? What do you believe is your purpose? If there's one thing you should take away from this personal race is that you must be brand-consistent across *all* of your social platforms or your message will attract little attention, or worse, attract the wrong attention.

I've been honing my personal brand for more than a decade. I never actually thought about it until my world as I knew it was pulled from under me. I was fired from what I considered to be a great job in a Fortune 100 company. *What was I going to do now? How could I make a living?* It was my first professional job and I was hired right out of college. I thought I was financially set for life. I actually never imagined that I would be fired from any company. I was devastated. I honestly didn't know where to begin. I had *zero* identity. My entire existence was centered around my employer. In hindsight, that rough patch became the most defining moment in my life and career. I went through the gamut of emotions from anxiety, to bouts of depression, and was stuck in "woe is me" conversations with close friends. After months of my griping and complaining, I guess my friend Glen couldn't take it anymore and he said, "Dude, you need to learn how to connect the dots. If you had not gotten fired, you would have never left!" His words struck a chord and instantly shifted my perspective. The truth is, Glen was right. I was extremely complacent and *never* considered my life outside of the corporate world receiving a bi-monthly paycheck, an expense account, bonuses, health insurance, and other company perks. Life was sweet and I envisioned climbing the corporate ladder. Although my reality seemed to make sense in hindsight, I was still scared of my future employability.

I believe part of my hesitation and fear was that I actually had multiple employment options. I did not want to get stuck in a position that would not allow me to move closer to my purpose. I wasn't sure how to dwindle down those options and make the right choice, especially in our democratized age of the internet where information is accessible to all. How do we figure out what career to settle for when we have multiple talents? Then I began thinking about the common themes in my life that the universe had been calling me to fulfill for years. It was if a light bulb came on and I began to see and understand those common themes.

I thought back to when I started working for that Fortune 100 company at 21 years old and I went on my first pharmaceutical sales call. As I approached the window, the secretary at the medical facility looked up at me and said, "Oh my God what are you doing in sales? You need to be in commercials doing voice overs." Has this ever happened to you? Has someone spotted a gift in you that you have been suppressing for years? How have you responded? Are you actualizing those gifts and talents that are innate? I imagine these types of close encounter gift-spotting happens to most of us. I know it can be daunting when you have multiple unique skillsets that are specifically made for you and only *you* to carry out.

It was eight years from my exchange with the medical secretary that my friend, Denise, a professional actress told me, "Syd you should be acting or doing voice-overs." I actually stayed silent for a while and forced myself to listen to my friends comment and to my gut. Over time, I took an honest evaluation of myself. I thought back to how I enjoyed journaling when I was younger. My parents, grandmother, and teachers always spoke of my desire to communicate, and how I commanded audiences at a young age. I had an insatiable desire to give a voice to those that did not have one. Now that I was unemployed, I had plenty of time to search and reevaluate my passion, purpose, and goals. Again, there were other employment opportunities, yet deep down, I always wanted to be an actor. My decision was made. I set my acting career path in motion. I got professional headshots and enrolled in professional acting classes in New York City.

After the first few weeks of classes, my nerves were a wreck. Every time the word "action" was uttered, I froze like a deer in headlights. My acting coach and others repeatedly said to me, "Syd, you have a great speaking voice. Why not try voice-overs?" At first, my ego was crushed. *Why hasn't anyone encouraged my acting dream? I can't be that bad, or am I?* Classes were over and I sulked for a few more weeks.

Another good friend convinced me to make a demo tape. I researched several studios and chose to work with a renowned studio also in New York. I was pleased with the demo and sent it out to agents. Within a few weeks, I was contacted by one of the top advertising agencies in the country. I was in awe. I went on auditions for an entire year and did *not* book one gig! I was deflated. I contacted my agent and told him that I was throwing in the towel. Acting didn't work out and voice-overs were not working out either. I'll never forget what he said to me that morning, "Syd, your problem is that you have to leave the audition at the audition. You keep taking it with you. Let it go. Move on. You will get the right gig. Hang in there! Just give me a few more weeks and you'll see."

I really wanted to work doing voice-overs so I had no choice but to hang in there and trust his instincts. After all, he was the expert in the field and I had not gotten my foot in the door. A few weeks later his assistant called me in for a national commercial for Dodge. I went in and read, "The all new Dodge Durango. New look. Big size. Smooth ride. Visit your local Dodge dealer today." A week after that, my agent called and informed me that it was down to me and one other person. I booked that commercial! Not only was it my first one, but it was also a big one. I became the voice of Dodge for the next 10 years. During that time I landed gigs for ESPN, Disney, and voiced over one thousand features. I now had this purpose-driven opportunity to learn brands from a different perspective, yet my common thread was in communicating. I started working on my vision and mission statement for what I wanted to do in the future. I went back to my childhood dream to be the voice for people who didn't have one. I envisioned myself as the go-to person to help build a bridge to knowledge, information, and brand importance in the U.S. and abroad. Think back to those recurring themes in your life. How tuned in are you to those themes? The universe is providing you with clues often and it is your job to plug into them so that you can actualize who you are and what you were called to do.

Working as a voice-over artist for hundreds of brands made me realize the power of brands in the marketplace but it also revealed the necessity of building a personal brand to be successful in whatever stage you are at in your career. Whether you are working a 9-to-5, an entrepreneur, a leader, or seeking to be a social media influencer, the stronger your personal brand the more likely you will have opportunities to grow into other areas of interest and be successful according to your terms.

As you begin to think and plan the days and months ahead, keep in mind the S.M.A.R.T **Brand Zones** to remain inspired and on track. The S.M.A.R.T acronym was first introduced in the early 1980s in a *Management Review* article by George T. Doran, and other business leaders as a goal-oriented management tool. Since then, some of the top business and thought leaders in the nation have developed their own *a la carte* version of S.M.A.R.T., to keep pace with business and societal changes.

In your brand-building race, you should prepare to start S.M.A.R.T:

1. **Be Specific:** Write clear, simple goals that will have a direct impact on your transformation. These goals must be important and significant to move forward. Sticking to your game plan is the key to success. Trying

something new every other month will alter your focus and deter your growth. For those of you looking to become Brand Rockstars, your goals need to be super specific! You must challenge yourself around doing more to narrow down exactly what you want to accomplish. Create your virtual vision board at this stage. Peruse the web and various apps that exemplify the lifestyle and career you desire.

2. **Make Measurable:** Another important factor will be creating measurable goals to track your progress and keep you motivated to reach the next milestone. In doing so, you can zero in on where you are, meet deadlines, and feel the rush of checking off the next progress point. Brand Rockstars are in to the data and data really matters. As you are tracking your success, break it up into quarters like the financial markets. Have you ever thought about breaking your life up into quarters? It is a great beginning to really see where you stand toward completion of your goals.

3. **Be Accountable:** Talk to colleagues and family members about your brand-building plan. Enlist their advice and feedback. Select one or two people you admire to be your accountability partners. These should be people who will push and stretch you to move out of your comfort zone.

4. **Be Realistic:** Set realistic goals for each milestone. Don't try to check off 10 tasks in one weekend. Remember, this new course of action is in addition to your current

career, family responsibilities, and other personal commitments and undertakings. Don't overburden yourself and then make excuses to quit. This is also a time to think outside the box and figure out what you can do better or differently than others.

5. **Be Timely**: Set a target date to achieve each goal. Having deadlines is critical to keeping a steady pace.

All of the S.M.A.R.T. factors are equally important and should be intentionally practiced for the best outcome. What's more, as you are delineating your goals and objectives, you should also take inventory of your body and mind consciousness. Our bodies are well-built machines. We need the right amount of sleep, proper food, nutrients, water, exercise, and mental and spiritual stimulation to be effective. If you are lacking in any of these areas, it's time to include any missing links into your daily regimen.

Using this book as a tool will be invaluable to your employability, growth, and success, regardless of your desired career field. It's time to stretch yourself. Improve your mental flexibility and build your personal brand at a pace that works perfectly for you and *only* you. The fastest runner doesn't always win the race. Even though the runner is fully prepared, it's all about being in the right place at the right time. If you stick to your plan, your chances of winning and achieving your personal best are bound to happen. Tighten your laces. The time is now. Prepare your mindset for a "new and improved" you. #Dream#Create #Win. Are you ready? Let's Go!

"Running is the greatest metaphor for life because you get out of it what you put into it."
– Oprah Winfrey

Pace 1: 0-30 DAYS

WIN THE MORNING

> *"We are what we repeatedly do.*
> *Excellence is not an act but a habit. "*
> **– Will Durant**

Before we embark upon any type of transformation of our mind, body, and spirit, to reveal our key brand attributes, we must first consider the deliberate steps needed to adequately prepare us for this personal goal-setting race. The warm-up was to get you fired up and motivated to win. But how long will your motivation last? As with most of us, we vacillate from one motivational moment or speaker to the next but never fulfilling our ultimate goal. I've done it more times than I care to share. Yet I realized that motivation wears off if there isn't anything deeper to sustain you so that you keep reaching for more. That's when I started thinking about habits and how developing a habit to start your day really goes beyond the warm-up. The habit, in essence, starts with the warm-up and ends with renewal on many levels.

I am a devout morning person. I absolutely love to be up early to get focused when the environment is quiet. It also helps me get a perspective of the day ahead. Early mornings helps to awaken our neurotransmitters to stimulate our brain for positive energy and activity. I have learned that if you shift slightly with small things it creates bigger, more meaningful habits in your life. Small shifts create big shifts. There were days where I drove a different route to work as my way of forcing my brain to think differently. I realized that the success of my day stemmed from my attitude in the morning. That is why I start each day with gratitude in meditation, which is about recognition and being thankful.

There are countless articles, books and scientific research that demonstrate the similarities in the morning routines of high achievers and groundbreaking leaders. The majority of these Type A personalities are up by 5 AM and have taken steps to prepare their mind and body for the day by exercising, meditating, yoga, and reading. All of these pre-workday rituals have helped them to achieve levels of excellence. I love the powerful quote mentioned above that is often credited to Aristotle but it was actually stated by Will Durant in his book, *The Story of Philosophy: The Lives and Opinions of the World's Greatest Philosophers,* where he summarizes Aristotle's works.

Over the years, many inspirational leaders have stated that it takes 21 days to form a habit. That "21 days" number was actually misquoted, as the original Dr. Maxwell Maltz said that it takes at *least* 21 days to form a habit and it was based on a few patient experiences. However, in 2009 another study was done by Phillippa Lally, a health psychology researcher at University College London. Dr. Lally's team found that on average, it takes more than two months before a new behavior becomes automatic — 66 days to be exact. So whether you are of the mindset that it takes 21 days or 66 days, the decisive point is that change will not happen overnight, and the more intentional you are about your actions, the higher your likelihood of success at making impactful changes.

Early Birds

"You will never change your life until you change your daily morning routine."

- *John Maxwell*

We're all familiar with the idiom, "the early bird catches the worm." As I have stated, successful people have a dynamic morning routine. They have mastered the art of taking charge of their morning to be the first to rise and be productive. I utilize a strategy where I am able to accomplish two days of productivity into one by rising very early. Of course, this may not work for everyone, but for me, the earlier the better. Then I meditate, head to the gym and focus on the day ahead. I want you to turn your Brand Rockstar behaviors into Brand Rockstar habits with the repetition of your effective morning routine.

One of my favorite books is *The Miracle Morning* by Hal Elrod. Hal literally transformed his life after recovering from a near death auto accident and a financial crisis by shifting his morning attitude and regimen. In his book, he encourages readers to win the day by having a powerful morning routine. Hal's philosophy is that if you want to take your life to the next level, the most important thing you can do is to improve how you start your day. Hal provides a 30-day challenge to change your life spiritually, emotionally and financially. First and foremost, you have to wake up earlier. Choose if you are going to meditate, exercise, or journal. The first few days will be unbearable. The next week will be uncomfortable. By the third week, you will feel unstoppable. For change to manifest, don't reward yourself when you reach the 30-day mark and don't take breaks in between. It's time to begin the positive self-talk: "I am necessary. The world needs what I have to offer. This is my journey and I determine the outcome. I can do this." The discipline and willpower start now. Make up your mind to win *every* morning and your first 30-days will make all the difference in the world. Don't hit the snooze button. Get up now!

Pace 2: 31-60 DAYS

Look Inside & Out

"Be yourself, everyone else is taken."
- Oscar Wilde

It can be exhausting and frustrating trying to actualize our true selves. Yet, what do we do when "our true self" is complex and made up of different sides? How do we choose which sides of ourselves we should be? Most of us have good and bad characteristics. Even if we fail to admit it, we all have a few bad ones. Building a powerful personal brand means harnessing all of your character traits and creating a signature of who you are. Hopefully, it should be an easy choice which side of your true self you need to highlight in the building process.

We are all unique and have the potential to accomplish great feats. Unfortunately, most of us fail to honestly seek within to discover our true selves. Many people simply lack knowledge of the importance of the process so they never strive beyond their comfort zone. Everyone needs to grow in some area of their lives. Therefore, in spite of all of the self-improvement courses or books people read on personal development, they will never actualize their true self and or grow into being a better person. I believe the primary reason for the lack of attainment is that most of us feel good about following the "in crowd" and using the self-help buzz words but never put in the required effort for meaningful change. You must respect the process. Change and betterment is a real process.

Another reason why people do not attain their goals is that they have a fear of executing. Yet execution really matters! It is vitally important to embrace your fear and push yourself beyond your wildest imagination. Stay in your own lane and use your unique talents. Don't be like the person coming into the gym and seeing someone in great shape and thinking you will be just like them in no time. I've been there. I was overweight and compared myself to every toned guy in the gym. After working with several trainers I realized that I needed to put in more effort. Change doesn't happen overnight. Like me, pace yourself. This is an ongoing process. My Grandma always said, "If you do not use your talents you will lose them." Go ahead and put the process and procedures into place so you can lean into your fears and execute.

Thinking back on when I got fired years ago, I was all over the place looking at others. I watched my friends buy houses and have kids, while I lived in an apartment. It was then that I learned that it truly is your *own* race and I cannot compare myself to others by creating faulty perceptions of what I should have or where I should be in my career. Instead, identify your skillsets and reach out to your closest friends to tell them your plans and brace yourself for honest feedback. I was really stuck with where to make my next move and voice-overs and acting were pulling my heartstrings. The vast majority of my friends were in agreement with my next move and said, "Absolutely, I don't know why have not done it before!" Reach out to people and put energy out there so you can help get direction on your next path. Even when we are not listening, the Universe is listening and watching our every move.

> **Brand Rockstar Tip:** Not only do Brand Rockstars execute on their action plans, but they also go back to their accountability partners and create a list of what is working and what is not working as well as ideas for improvement. They then reconfigure that list as often as possible. It does not have to be pretty. I can tell you that my lists and notes were messy but I saved them and referred to them often. You need these types of mile markers to show you how to move from A to B and what shift needs to happen to ensure all your dots are connected.

Like anything worth striving for, you really have to want it from within. Just how bad do you want to build your brand? How important is it for you to change your current lifestyle? Usually, when I begin a conference, I poll the audience with two questions. First I ask, "How many people have a personal brand?" About 70% of the people in the room hands go up. Then I ask, "How many people believe they have a *powerful* personal brand?" Like clockwork, all of the hands go down.

This tells me two things: i) people are aware that they need a personal brand and ii) they are in this session to learn how to make it stronger and take it across the globe.

I often remind people that this is an individual race that starts with you and ends with you. Think of yourself as one of the horses at the starting gate of the Kentucky Derby. Like each horse, you have on the sturdy leather blinder around your head to prevent you from seeing the distractions behind you or to your left and right. With no distractions, you have zero excuses for not finishing strong. Work hard to become the best possible *you* that you can be. Do you believe that you are worth it? It's like the old adage, "Wherever you go, there you are." In essence, there is no escaping you. This life-changing race requires you to accentuate your positives.

Changing your outward appearance, your address, or learning a new language can help improve your confidence. I challenge you to begin to work from the inside out, rather than the outside in, as the outward is too subjective, and you may never feel whole. Nevertheless, if there is another look that you want to strive for, then go for it! Review your virtual vision board. For me, even though I could not afford it, I cut out styles and other items that were indicative of the lifestyle I wanted. I was actualizing and forecasting the life that I knew would eventually come to pass. I challenge you to do the same.

Recognizing that I am a constant work in progress, I create a record every day of three things that I did well and three things I could do better. I also keep a file of articles categorized by subjects that inspire me, challenge me, and allow me to think differently. Then I try to keep all of these materials organized for future reference and there are a ton of tools and apps to help with organization. Choose which one(s) work best for your needs. For those of you who struggle with organization, find people to help you get it done. Think about that person who pushes you to go to the next level. It can be someone close to you or someone who you know cursory. If you are like me, I can tell you that being pushed is not comfortable. I recall hanging up the phone with my friend Glen after a tough conversation and I was not feeling great. It was not pretty. He forced me to be more self-reflective and take personal accountability to get into my brand zone with determination and measurable steps.

You were not born a brand, but you can become one. Everyone is not meant to be a powerful brand. Keep in mind that using your unique skillsets and talents is one thing, but being a brand is another. The good news is that you can take on the role as your own personal trainer towards your development. Of course, you can hire a middleman like a life coach or other personal growth expert, but start out on your own terms and see where it takes you. Don't get too distracted by what someone else thinks your route should be. It's really within your control. As part of your pacing routine, you will be required to honestly look deep within, to find out who you really are, versus what you currently do for a living.

INNER VOICE
"Don't let the noise of other people's opinions drown out your inner voice."
- Steve Jobs

We are all spiritual beings. Regardless of your religion or belief system, you are equipped with an inner voice that constantly speaks into your thoughts. Often times it can be similar to an interruption. Don't believe me? Think about all those times when you were driving in your car or engaged in a conversation, and all of a sudden that voice inside told you that you left the oven on or you forgot to lock the front door. Rest assured, that's your inner voice alerting you to a situation. That voice can stop you dead in your tracks in your daily life. Suffice it say, our internal make-up is much more powerful and important than our external appearance.

I cannot overstate the point that building your personal brand will require a great deal of reflection and listening to your inner voice. It should be your "go to" voice that guides your game plan. Trust it. Your search within should help you discover your core personal values and passions. Most people can draft a laundry list of values, yet they quickly change their position under pressure to go with the flow and appease the majority. Still, others actually know their values or passion, yet are too embarrassed to share it. Chances are, they expressed their feelings in the past to someone close to them who probably asked, "How are you going to make money doing that?" Don't be discouraged if your passion is unconventional. The person firing the starting gun is not aiming at you, but that blaring sound is to remind you to run with everything you've got. If your "thing" keeps you up at night, continue to run with it. The finish line is wherever you want it to be after there is true progress. You are in control. Make it count once and for all.

"Ego is the biggest enemy of humans."
- Rig Veda

Listening to our inner voice is not as easy as it sounds. For me, I have found my inner voice competing with my ego, and sometimes other voices. Our ego has a way of duping us from reality. The more time we spend in silence and stillness, the greater our chances of discerning the inner voice to lead us down a fulfilling path of self-discovery. It takes patience, practice, and commitment. Be completely honest with yourself. Are you up for the challenge? Consider these **Brand Zones** to help reveal your true self.

1. **Identify:** What three words best characterize you? It is essential for you to identify who you are through an honest assessment. Not only should you list three words, but you should speak with three or four people that know you well enough to provide feedback. Compare notes.

2. **Describe:** What core competencies can you attach to those words? It is important to attach skill sets to your descriptors. One of the disconnects with the current job market continues to be an applicant's lack of tangible skills. For example, (i) your brand transcends your job; what would you be known for outside of your employer?; (ii) learn and understand your value proposition; what makes you marketable? Valuable to the company?; and (iii) what critical company solutions will you solve? Answering these questions is a clear jump-start to hone, tweak or increase your skills.

3. **Apply:** How can you apply these redefined skill sets to finish your race? What, if any, additional skills can you add to increase your likelihood of success?

OUTER APPEARANCE

Working on yourself from within is an ongoing process. Over time, it will become easier to get into the "moment" and really run with the energy you need to win any race. Others should notice a difference in you. They will see that you have taken their constructive feedback to heart and are pacing yourself with a work-in-progress mindset.

With your inner mind-stretching and shaping up, it's time to shift your focus to the outside— your outward appearance. Do you believe the saying, "If you look good, you feel good?" I do! Looking good exudes confidence. When you have confidence in your appearance and clothing, you are operating with a winning attitude. A positive attitude is just as becoming like a "to die for" outfit. It will open the gates of optimism as you approach daily tasks and give you the confidence to believe that your efforts will be successful.

In fact, looking good may even make you feel happy. Of course, each person's definition of happiness is relative to her circumstances, yet at the end of the day, all of the work involved in re-discovering your true self is about finding the main triggers to happiness. Have you ever seriously thought about what makes you happy on the outside? Life is full of challenges, however, choose to be happy and rid yourself of negative thoughts and people. Write down the following **Brand Zones** and see if any of them resonate with you. Create your own list as well.

i) What makes you smile?
ii) What do you enjoy doing above everything else?
iii) What subject keeps you talking for hours on end?

By now you should have figured out part of the secret. It's like having a virtual vision board of the internal buttons that make you move. Building your brand should feel like a purging process— out with the old, in with the new. I've talked to so many people who are uncomfortable setting aside time to focus on themselves. Some see it as a sign of selfishness. I personally view it as a sign that you have finally put a stake in the ground and no longer put others and everything else *before* your needs. We all must get to this point, or we will wake up one day and realize that we have lived our lives according to others' expectations and by their rules. Don't let third parties' thoughts or feelings about what you should or should not do, hinder your preparation or progress.

One big hindrance to growth is the comparison game. It is a total waste of time to compare yourself to others. Although we are all on our own journey, we can also be our own worst enemy. Remember the horse in the Kentucky Derby with blinders? I mentioned comparisons earlier and I am reiterating it again because it was a real challenge for me. I wish I had this knowledge in my early 20's. I was fixated on, who had a better apartment? Who had the bigger title? Who made the most money? Later, I found out that these things were irrelevant and the true purpose of my inner being was to add value to whatever *I* was doing with what I had. When I seriously made this mindset shift, I was able to focus more on my own goals and excel to levels beyond my wildest dreams.

It's Never Too Late

Late bloomers line up and start now! I am so encouraged when I read stories of those who took the leap of faith and went after their passion later in life. Musical genius Mozart spent years unfulfilled and underpaid early in his career and he knew that if he had more free time to devote to his music it would pay off. He quit his job ad worked on his music and his level of mastery is beyond compare. Not to mention the great philosopher Aristotle believed that one of our most important discoveries is to become conscious of our skills and talents and then using our resources to bring them to fruition to find fulfillment. In fact, Aristotle did not start writing philosophy until in his 50s. What has been holding you back? Your age? Your job? Your family? Don't let past stops and starts hold you back. Your race starts with you and ends with you.

In his book *Late Bloomers,* author Rich Karlgaard makes a great argument about our culture's obsession with early achievement. In striving for optimal results early it discourages us from pursuing our passions as we get too focused on becoming an expert at one thing that we let our other interests fall by the wayside. No matter how successful you have been at one thing, its never too late to tap into the other "what if" thing that keeps you up at night. Set goals for the activities and steps to do what's been gnawing at you for years. Who knows? There could be larger than life brand brewing inside that has been waiting to come out. It's true that with age their is wisdom and more self-knowledge from experiencing life. Karlgaard writes, the "ages 40 to 64 constitute a unique period where one's creativity and experience combine with a universal human longing to make our lives matter." Thus, once you make up your mind to change course, it could take years to reach your destination but the most important thing is that you reached your goal and won!

RUNNER'S HIGH

Runner's High is a term used to define an exhilarating and euphoric feeling that overtakes you after consistent running. It occurs when our bodies naturally produce endorphins that kick in when we are feeling emotional or pain.

I believe you should strive for a "Branding High" where your actions and behavior are moving you toward actualizing your goals. *What #BrandRockstars do!* Review your Brand Zones. Be diligent. Complete at least one task on your brand-building transformation list each week. Push yourself, but don't create unrealistic expectations that will deter you from moving forward. Sometimes it takes one small step like an encouraging word to provide the momentum you need. Keep striding until you reach that "Runner's High."

One of the things that I personally do twice a year is a 360-degree assessment from at least four people that I trust to deliver honest and constructive feedback. One year, the best piece of advice that I was ever given was to keep a journal or another medium to track successes and failures. Journaling allowed me to be free to write about my goals, ambitions. It was a great outlet for increasing my self-awareness, as well as managing and expressing my emotions. The greatest predictor of future performance is past behavior. For the past few years, I finish each day by taking an assessment of what I did well and what I could do better. Another thing that I am mindful of is that fact that there is power is saying hello. One practice that I utilize is to say Happy Monday or Happy Tuesday for each day of the week. People begin to associate you based on your salutations. I was deliberate in associating my name with positivity. Positivity is contagious!

Self-awareness is the real key to taking control of your life. It must be an intentional effort on your part to take time out of your day to objectively document your actions and inaction. Journaling your hits and misses is a fantastic way to stay accountable to yourself and your goals. This practice has proved to be an invaluable marker for my self-actualization and growth. Take these simple steps to help increase your self-awareness:

- Create a record of your day.
- Compile inspiring photos, articles, or quotes to spark creativity.
- Brainstorm new ideas more effectively.
- Stay organized.
- Be accountable.
- Put forth the real effort to achieve your stated goals.

Millennials: Gen Y.

How Do You Measure Up?

> *"You have to have a canon so the next generation can come along and explode it."*
> *- Henry Louis Gates*

Personal branding is a hot topic of conversation amongst Millennials. Why is branding so important to them? Research shows that the Millennial generation (aka Gen Y), those born between the early 1980s and 1990s are the fastest growing demographic in today's workforce. Technology alone is keeping this group well-informed and connected to the world. Those of us that make up Gen Y tend to view the future with great optimism and are eager to share their multi-talents. This "sky's the limit" outlook fuels their desire to explore new opportunities often and affords them the opportunity to work for several companies throughout their career. This is a vast difference from Baby Boomers and Gen X, who more than likely worked for the same or a handful of companies before retirement.

I think what I find the most interesting about Gen Y and X is that technology has made it extremely easy to create a personal brand, yet so many of this generation says it's hard to do. I think it's pretty easy for anyone to set up an Instagram page or LinkedIn account. Even though the metrics change often, for the most part, navigating through this process is still user-friendly.

One of the reasons many people have trouble creating successful brands is that they think exposure translates into monetary success. Yes, exposure is great and can lead to name recognition, yet revenue generation is not a given. For one thing, clarity around your personal brand is vital. That's why self-reflection of exactly what you are doing as it relates to your Intelligence Quotient (IQ) helps position you against your competition. Always keep in mind that there is a time and place for everything, and it is not what you say but how you say it! Therefore, it is in your best interest to be a lot savvier in crafting your story. Stay in your lane. There is a lane for every topic out there yet everything does not need to be said by you.

Most people are familiar with IQ which is a person's cognitive ability to learn. IQ is usually measured by testing or even a person's grade point average. However, EQ, your Emotional Quotient or EI, Emotional Intelligence deals with your ability to monitor your own emotions as well as the emotions of others. Having good emotional foundation will help you connect with others and empathize more, as well as become more authentic and healthy.

My goal is to really focus on Brand Rockstars with the EI to understand who you are speaking to and why your subject matter is important. How do you understand who you are speaking to? Anyone can make an argument or study for anything and even create findings with real data. I've learned that if you have the ability to vacillate who you are, and you are using the DISC assessment tool mentioned below, you are operating in Brand Rockstar territory and not just on your personal brand. Focus on using your Emotional Intelligence Quotient (EIQ) to really connect to everyone you are speaking to especially in person as you want to actualize and genuinely connect one-on-one. Make sure you know who you are before you can speak to other people, and again, DISC is a powerful tool to help you to do that.

Gen Y'ers are seeking to be ahead of the curve and part of the next best thing. This group has become walking billboards for major product and service advertising. Whether it's the new iPhone, technological gadget, or fashion trend, a Gen Y'er will be front and center and post their wares on Instagram for the world to take notice. In addition, it appears that this group is comfortable communicating and speaking out for what they believe in, so the likelihood of success in using their brand to inspire and motivate others to act is definitely in their favor.

Previous generations have been exposed to the Myers-Briggs personality type indicator tests, which were first published in 1943. Over the years, the Myers-Briggs tests have been modified and although it received backlash, it is still used in employment, marriage counseling, and other self-improvement settings. Social media has also contributed to the need to "find oneself" and every day a new survey appears on one of the popular sites to help you determine your personality, mood color, compatibility, and other characteristics.

More important, there is an increasing popularity in self-help books, as well as life coaches popping up by the thousands. Everyone is in this constant cycle to better themselves both inwardly and outwardly. There are new personality and career-related tests based on documented research that continues to peak the interests of the Gen Y workforce future. My advice is to continue to fuel the desire to be better but don't go overboard. Make steady, consistent improvements over time so that they last.

The DiSC° Method

As a certified DiSC leader, I have taught hundreds of people this method and clearly see the benefits of this type of personal assessment tool to help you work towards building your brand. DiSC is used to help improve productivity, teamwork, and communication. I enjoy working with the DiSC method because it is non-judgmental and really engages honest group discussion as it relates to an individual's behavioral differences. Unlike the Myers-Briggs assessment, DiSC focuses more on understanding a person's behavior and temperament. Use of this method provides you with the ability to vacillate between who you are in order to speak the same language of your target audience, colleague, or customer. More and more Millennials are creating their DiSC profiles to help them see the big picture of how they really think, act, and interact with others.

As a young corporate executive, I learned the DISC model from a few of the original creators. At the outset, I was fascinated by the power you could harness from self-awareness. I remember teaching a class for DISC and the vast majority of the attendees were older than me and they immediately asked, "How will this help me and what does it have to do with my sales goals?" I explained that if you really know who you are, you will sell better, act better and interact better with others, not just from a business perspective, but personally. Brand Rockstars not only answer the questions they refine their answers and work on ways to become better. I still create weekly lists on what I did well and what I can improve upon. I focus on two or three things based on feedback and I aggregate the trends to see how I can improve in that area.

DiSC became real to me and I studied my assessment as I was preparing for my own self-test. One Christmas, I engaged in DiSC assessments on my entire family. It was eye-opening. As a result, communications improved because we were all able to appreciate and have a better understanding of the different words and actions that we inherently respond to based on our personalities. In addition, I secretly created an internal game to guess others DiSC position in an attempt to communicate with them more effectively. After over 10 years of utilizing the model, I have garnered an amazing ability to communicate with people from all walks of life.

"Knowing others is intelligence; knowing yourself is true wisdom, Mastering others is strength; mastering yourself is true power."
- The Tao Te Ching, Lao Tzu

DiSC looks at the following personality traits:

Dominance – direct, strong-willed and forceful

Influence – sociable, talkative and lively

Steadiness – gentle, accommodating and soft-hearted

Conscientiousness – private, analytical and logical

Your ability to vacillate in and out of one DiSC position to the other is where your strength lies. Each DiSC position has equal weight; no trait is better than the other. As you build your personal brand, really consider the importance of each trait, and how you can demonstrate it according to each prong to your target audience. Consumers will expect your message to be confident and relatable to their lifestyle. Show them what you're working with so that they come back again and again.

For those working in teams or seeking to build a team, DiSC profiles can help everyone gain a better understanding of team members as well as assist in handling conflict and stressful situations. The DiSC questionnaire is written in easy to understand phrases to give participants a broader meaning behind the questions. The test is taken online and there are really no right or wrong answers. Knowing your DiSC profile is invaluable as you set out on building your brand. Tools are irrelevant if you do not apply them. If your employer does not offer this assessment, it is definitely worth scouting out on your own. After all, it is up to you to put in the time, effort, and finances to run your race in this ever-changing market-place.

Your Value

The more unique and valuable your brand, the better avenues you will have to grow or use your brand to leverage other op-portunities. A huge factor in determining your value is your belief in your abilities. Early in my branding strategist career I did not have enough confidence to ask for money for the value I brought to clients. It was one of the biggest mistakes I ever made. I was so focused on getting my name out there and I loved what I was doing, but I did not equate dollars to my value. Granted I was traveling and all of my expenses were paid, but at the end of the day, if you are not making money it is a hobby. Having a unique skillset is a value that people pay for, so make your value clear in the beginning.

Demonstrating value has to be effectively communicated to your target market and to yourself. Are you feeding yourself empowering stories? Do you believe that you have what it takes to succeed? Your belief in yourself is critical and it is the predicate to action which will be discussed further as you continue to pace yourself. Be authentic, honest and clear about your value. Fuel up on positive moments and reframe any negative narratives of your past.

I'm often surprised by how many people cannot effectively tell their story. Honing your story is the most powerful adage to separate your brand from the competition. I actually practiced in the mirror telling my story of growing up in Philadelphia to myself. In doing so, it helped me think through key points and potential questions and answers from the audience. My family did not have great means when I was growing up. We lived in a small two-bedroom house but there was a strong sense of community. People supported each other and wanted to see their neighbors win and succeed.

Everyone's story is different even if two people lived in the same neighborhood or household. Each person brings a unique perspective. When drafting your story, lean into tell it from a position of power. Make sure you highlight challenges growing up, traumatic situations, and how you overcame the adversity. People want to connect and follow someone who has overcome obstacles. You should also research brand leaders that you admire to learn how they built strong brands.

At the end of the day, your race revolves around your uniqueness and value. Everyone has a methodology for how they operate. For me, it is a process of how I think through things and structure problems. I tend to be a problem-solver which is a great asset. Whether you work for a company, are an entrepreneur, or creating your online brand, people are looking for solutions. How can you help them remedy a situation? Alleviate stress? Find balance? Are you adding value to others by offering information without seeking anything in return?

"All great ideas need an ecosystem to materialize."

When I started contributing to brandingmag.com, I knew that I wanted to be seen as a thought leader. I decided that the best way to become known was that I needed to speak with industry leaders. I realized that many leaders would not speak to me, and I didn't care. I had a plan. I came up with idea for C-Suite and after I had been writing for a year, I pitched it to the owners of brandingmag and over two dozen C-Suites later, we are moving into other iterations as well as expanded into a podcast. This is what I mean by thinking outside of the box. Create ideas from scratch and have the confidence to execute. The C-Suite articles have helped me to grow my personal brand by creating trust and credibility for nearly three years of consistent production.

Now would be a good time to write down examples of problems you faced and how you solve them. I wrote an article in *Forbes* on making a critical decision in a defining moment in your life. Think back to a time when you had to make two or three decisions that you never thought you'd have to make. What factors led to your decision-making? Are you better off since the decision was made? Is there something you wish you had done differently?

Since you are running as a solo entity, think of your value as a company's core competency; that unique, uncommon ability and quality that only you have. Your personalized core competency is what will set you apart to deliver your best from a services perspective to your internal and external customers.

Remember, there can only be one you, so others cannot copy or duplicate what you bring to the table. In order to run ahead of the pack in your area of expertise, train hard and get out of the starting block by:

- Focusing on your key strengths and take continuing education courses, job shadowing, or seek a mentor to further enhance that strength;
- Keeping an eye on industry trends, experts in your field, and build alliances with third-party organizations to help broaden your reach; and
- Fine-tuning your DiSC personality traits to ensure they align with your brand and the message you want to convey.

Brand Zones

We all have core competencies that make us who we are. Begin to brainstorm and make a list of your goals for the coming year. It is vitally important to assess your skills accordingly and hold yourself accountable.

i) What were some of your goals and objectives from your employer performance review?

ii) What do you do better than others?

iii) What tasks are you doing that are time-consuming? Can someone take on those responsibilities?

iv) Do you have the current and appropriate certifications? What new certifications might be needed?

v) Who can help you identify and complete them?

vi) Have you sought honest 360-degree feedback?

vii) Make a list of the personal brands that you admire. Trace their success and see if there are similar avenues for you to embark upon.

RUNNER'S HIGH

The whole purpose of running your race is to set yourself apart from the pack. Competition for jobs, opportunities, and other leverage-building events will continue to challenge your patience, stamina, and talents. Believe in your abilities. Celebrate your uniqueness. Whether you are in administration, marketing, sales, or technology, stretch yourself to find your niche to offer others.

I love reading true stories of successful people who were wandering down mundane paths with no passion and ultimately awoke or had a once in a lifetime opportunity to demonstrate their gifts. Most brand books focus on top corporate leaders such as Steve Jobs, Jeff Bezos, Bill Gates, and Oprah Winfrey. Granted, all of these leaders have great stories of rising to the top, but I am drawn to the more quirky ones like the infamous, Walt Disney. Most people don't know that Walt was a newspaper editor. He was fired from his job because "he lacked imagination and had no good ideas." Another example is one of my favorite comedians and talk show hosts, Ellen DeGeneres.

Before becoming a household name, she was a paralegal and oyster shucker! Then there are my heroes, Tim and Nina Zagat. As a total foodie, I found inspiration in their stories as Yale law graduates and corporate lawyers for over 20 years. They left their stable careers to create the premiere dining survey service, ZAGAT. Thank you, Tim and Nina, I'm not sure how I could ever manage the restaurant maze without you! Although cliche, it's really not where you start, it's where and how you finish.

I believe the best aspect of these brand runner's stories is that once they hit their stride, they never looked back! How you measure up to others is not as important as how you see yourself in the future. Think big, work hard, and build on a strong foundation. Are you running your best race? Really think about who you are and what you offer that will make people want to connect with you. Get out your journal and write your story and make it plain and simple. Envision yourself standing in a room sharing your story. You have to embrace fear and execute with *your* story. Answer these questions:

1) What is your story?

2) What were your challenges growing up?

3) What were your challenges in college, work or at home?

4) How did you overcome them?

5) What was your defining moment to do better?

6) How can you help others?

7) What problems can you solve?

Pace 4: 91-120 DAYS

The Course Ahead

---

*"Everyone thinks of changing the world, but no
one thinks of changing himself."*
- Leo Tolstoy

Whenever I think of change, my thoughts turn to the best-selling book, *Who Moved My Cheese?*, by Dr. Spencer Johnson. This book was one of the first required reading assignments in undergrad at the prestigious Florida A&M University, School of Business and Industry taught by Dean Mobley. Although *Who Moved My Cheese?* has been required reading for decades in schools and business, the universal message still applies today. For the nutshell version, the story is written in an allegory and cheese is used as a metaphor for change to help readers see that adapting to change in their lives is necessary for survival. Dr. Johnson used four main characters: two mice, Sniff and Scurry, and two little people, Hem and Haw. Each character is unique with their own distinct personality, as each one of us.

The little people were content when they found the biggest piece of cheese they had ever stumbled upon in their maze.

They had no desire to *ever* search for cheese again and feared life-altering change. Operating outside of their comfort zone was not an option. Sound familiar? The mice, on the other hand, were more open-minded, and were on a constant search for more cheese, especially when they realized that the supply was dwindling down to nothing. The main point Dr. Johnson made in his groundbreaking book is that change is inevitable, and we all must deal with it, even if we do so differently.

Who Moved My Cheese? will eventually change to *Who Moved My Mobile Phone?* because we cannot do anything without our cell phone. We need to be forced to think differently and we can do so without a cell phone. You must spend more time thinking about who you are and where you want to go. There are great articles written about the importance of starting your day with calmness and reflection without looking at your cell phone as soon as you wake up.

As we shift to video podcast and technology improves our challenge with that is there is a lot of competition and how do you navigate in your field? I believe execution is key. A lot of people do not execute, instead, they talk about execution and approach change with fear or "woe is me" attitude. Early on, fear of being out front and leading the brand-building pack paralyzed me. Looking back I should have started video two years ago but I was stuck in my story and my why, but I had a passion to help, communicate and inform. So instead of operating at the forefront, I was comfortable in the foreground and shifted my focus on being an industry leader by increasing my knowledge. I went on LinkedIn and targeted every industry leader from the Middle East, Africa, Europe and literally around the globe. Having an ear to international trends allowed me to travel and speak in countries I once dreamed of visiting.

I still read 10-15 articles from my Google alerts each day and when I find a solution to an article that I read, I offer it to the writer or the organization. Branding is a cross-industry and I am passionate around knowledge-sharing and service. So when I go to a restaurant and tweet about an experience I ask others for comments. Even when I don't agree with the comment, I am satisfied that I gave my perspective and solution around the issue.

Therefore, as industries change based on consumer need, demand, and other social and economic factors, you also need to change with the times. Be open to increasing your knowledge and skills to make you an invaluable asset for your own company, your next employer, or your next business opportunity. Don't miss out on the shift to video podcasts as technology evolves so you stay ahead of the curve. There is no time to sit in the stands watching others run by. You must be open to change.

Changing Industry Sectors

To a large extent, technology alone is dictating the demand for change in nearly every industry sector. The need for one-on-one contact with companies is becoming less critical. We can manage all of our appointments, banking, investing, shopping and any other personal needs online, and in most cases on our smartphones. With this growing trend, many industries will do away with hundreds or thousands of employees sitting behind cubicles handling customer service issues or other traditional in-house back office or desk duties. Across industry, authenticity will always prevail in the ever-shifting landscape.

Staying ahead of the curve requires you to be focused on the trends and future outlook for your industry sector. Whether you are in the public or private sector, finance, real estate, technology, healthcare, or manufacturing industries, keeping abreast and continuing your education and expertise will be the key to winning your race. **Think different:** easy in theory, hard in practice. Go back and think of how you solve problems. The one thing that will never change is the need to solve problems. Stay solutions focused. Uber, Airbnb you don't necessarily need to disrupt but think of a solution. Start where YOU are....what problems do you recognize? What is your solution?

i) **Banking/Finance** - Most of us have already seen a huge shift in banking on our smartphones. The need to enter a 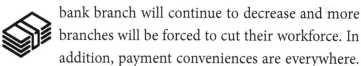 bank branch will continue to decrease and more branches will be forced to cut their workforce. In addition, payment conveniences are everywhere. Consumers no longer have to use their bank to perform monetary transactions. They can use payment vehicles like PayPal, Square, Cash App, Zelle, and several others. How can you position your financial knowledge to enhance your brand? Are you a broker? Customers are turning to online banking and information as well as setting up online brokerage accounts instead of seeking personal financial advice. If this is your career field, stay on top of the current research and trends to find your financial niche to differentiate yourself from your peers.

Financial experts agree that one major transformation within the banking industry will be developing partnerships or expanded collaboration with outside organizations. Banks and financial institutions will invest in innovation and personalized customer experiences. What about the cashless store's buzz? Cashless society? Well, according to recent reports, Sweden will be the first cashless society in 2023. Aside from technology, there will continue to be a need for human connection and experiences in the financial industry. How can you help? Where do you fit in within the broader financial landscape?

ii) **Marketing** - Providing a memorable experience for customers requires those in marketing careers to constantly stay ahead of the curve using the latest in technology. Educating yourself on the Omnichannel business model will be beneficial, as it crosses various industries including banking, retail, healthcare, and government. This model allows customers input to be fine-tuned and tailored for their likes and needs. It is a multichannel sales vehicle that offers consumers a seamless shopping experience, whether they're shopping online from a desktop or mobile device, by telephone, or in a brick-and-mortar store. It gives customers direct involvement in an organization's product and service offerings 24/7. In addition, learning additional techniques and uses for video to communicate your message will be invaluable, as video continues to be in demand—YouTube, Facebook Live, Twitter and mobile video uploads on Instagram will be around for a while. If you are a marketer, measuring your strategies will be the key to customer retention and referrals. Having a working knowledge of the digital channels and platforms gives you insight and access to data. Consider ways to use micro-influencers to help you position your brand for your target audience. Marketing to the right audience will be key as the younger generation, Gen Z is more engaged on Instagram, Snapchat and YouTube as opposed to Facebook and Twitter. Be flexible and open to learning and using new technology, marketing apps, voice apps and strategies to broaden your customer engagement with more service offerings than the rest of the pack.

Do you have a product or service to market? This is a time to take risks even if you have a 9-to-5. Your personal experiences and lessons learned in marketing your own product or service can be a huge commodity in attracting similarly situated customers and set you apart from others in the field.

iii) **Real Estate** - The real estate industry will always have peaks and valleys as it is heavily dependent on the economy and the U.S. government-backed financial system. However, this also is an industry where technology has made a huge impact. Realtors can provide virtual tours of homes, buyers can perform instant mortgage calculations, price comparisons and gain virtually everything they need to know about homes and neighborhoods. Forward thinkers like Compass CEO Robert Reffkin, are working to make home purchaser's experience a one stop shop. Reffkin envisions his company as the "place where everything is in one platform; mortgage, title, insurance, escrow, inspectors, move-in services, everything in one place creating harmony."[1]

Trulia, the real estate search engine changed the home-buying playing field. They formed a partnership with Hip Hop legend MC Hammer which allows homeowners to "Hammerfy" their home search. Since home buying can be a stressful experience, Trulia wants to make the experience fun and entertaining. Homebuyers are required to answer a few questions about what they are looking for and the system has over 3,000 combinations of tunes and videos that highlight their name and style while Hammer and his dancers sing tunes related the homebuyer's criteria. The videos and songs can be shared with others. Look for other real estate search engines to partner with celebrities to offer similar consumer experiences.

If you are in real estate, continue to expand your reach using automation for emails and texting of new listings and helpful information. Ensure that you have a brand-worthy presence on all major social media platforms. Always use professional photos and videos when featuring a property—the more videos the better. Become an expert about the communities you serve and network with other business owners in order to build trust, as opposed to just plastering your photo all around town. Be authentic. Be resourceful. Be the agent that people trust. Your brand will go far beyond the agency.

iv) **Technology** - For those of you in a technological field or looking to go into this field, opportunities to learn, grow and be on the cutting edge of the consumer experience are endless. It really doesn't matter what career field you are in, creating an app or new lifestyle practice can be fulfilling. There are vast opportunities to enroll in technology courses online, whether for a specific degree or continuing education certifications. Even if you are not a techie, it can be helpful to learn new software or other technological innovations in communication or consumer engagement.

As it stands, the ongoing technological advances in wireless technology have created a consumer demand for lightning speed in everything that we do. We want it now and it *must* be faster than yesterday and even faster tomorrow. Just consider the great lengths that Verizon Fios spends in every communications medium now known to man, to convey how much faster their internet package is compared to the competition. I often think to myself, *do I really need to know how to make vegetable lasagna in twenty seconds versus forty?* Maybe. Maybe not.

For years, brand strategists have honed in on the importance of creating your verbal and visual brand to set you apart from a crowded market. However, moving forward, we need to add another layer of the senses in reaching the consumer. Experts now say that icons and symbols are great, but "earcons" also need to be considered. What does your brand sound like? How do people feel when they *hear* a representation of your band? Sound plays an equally important role in how you express yourself in the marketplace, so make sure your videos and music are reflective of your brand vision and purpose.

In addition, Intelligence Agents like Alexa, Siri and Google Assistant, have become the "go to" systems of information for millions of households. These devices have become like family members with users of all ages talking to them and receiving advice throughout the day. Experts predict that the trend for these types of Intelligence Agents will become smarter and process information faster, in order to anticipate the needs and wants of consumers.

Fast. Faster. Fastest. These should *not* be the adjectives cluttering your mind as you formulate your personal brand-building strategy. Put aside thoughts of winning the 100-meter dash. Instead, approach the start line with confidence and diligent preparation towards finishing your first marathon. Completing 26.2 miles is no small feat. It actually sets you apart from the majority. In fact, according to *Runner's World*, only five percent of the U.S. population have run a marathon. The sooner you commit to a weekly brand-building schedule, the more likely you will be ready to run the big race towards your ultimate purpose. In this case, "running" your own race is the goal to make yourself more marketable and ultimately fulfilled in your next endeavor.

v) **Personal Branding** - Your branding strategy is cyclical. As long as you are consistent and take the right steps to stay ahead of the curve, you should be well positioned to compete. Some analysts have stated that personal branding is dead. I beg to differ. Your personal brand is not solely based on your perspective, but largely on the perceptions of others. It is the aggregate of the positive and negative as seen largely through the lens of others. Revisit your story and your unique value to the marketplace. What do you stand for? What life lessons shaped you? What will others say about your work ethic or integrity?

Why choose You?
What is your value proposition?
Does your profile clearly articulate?
Do you have a content strategy?
Do you have a content calendar?
Are YOU consistent?

When you really think about it, you are your own CEO. How you live out your daily life is a total reflection of your values and onlookers will equate your personal characteristics with that of your company or the company you work for. Have you ever noticed that when a top leader has a personal misstep or challenge that the company's stock price drops? To the public, if you are in a leadership position, you and the company are one and the same. Therefore, be authentic in every area where you are engaging others, especially on social media. Also, seek to promote others and refrain from self-promotion. Add value to others and connect with a cause that demonstrates your beliefs.

In addition, there is a personal branding strategy that can earn branders six-figure incomes being social media influencers. These branders usually have followers of at least 100K and they are used by companies as a marketing strategy to influence those branders followers to buy a certain product or service.

What do influencers do? Influencers tout themselves as experts in their craft of promoting other brands. In doing so, influencers become popular brands in their own right. Celebrities, athletes, as well as CEOs of large companies quickly become social media influencers the moment they open an account in the popular sites. That's because their brand has already been established based on their movie or television fame, athletic accomplishments or company's track record. If you desire to be an influencer you must be ready to put in the work to post a lot of quality content daily. The more you post that strikes a chord with your target audience, the more followers you gain. The key is to be authentic, respond to people who reach out to you, and post as much original creative content to attract people. In doing so, brands will find your personal brand to connect with to promote their product or service. As with anything, start small and work on a strategy to build your influencer brand that highlights your personality and core values.

I spoke with the CEO and founder of HYPR, Gil Eyal. Gil has built a client base of over 100 Fortune 500 brands and 100 of the biggest advertising and PR agencies in the world, including LVMH, Next Models, Levi Strauss, Hearst Magazines, Calvin Klein, Time Inc., and Estée Lauder. Therefore, he is used to working closely with celebrities. He was also the COO of the photo-sharing app Mobli, where he became a trailblazer in the influencer marketing space – recruiting over 120 celebrities including stars like Leonardo DiCaprio and Serena Williams.

It was great to hear Gil explain why a large following (audience) doesn't necessarily translate to meaningful engagement and what makes a successful influencer marketing campaign. Finally, he explained the micro-influencer role, and why they have been gaining such an increased presence on social media (including what brands should know before partnering with one). Gil shared a wealth of information that can help you

I'm a big believer in the concept that influencer marketing is a form of marketing and the same fundamental rules that apply to traditional marketing should apply to influencer marketing. There's this fascination in the industry with engagement levels (e.g., how many people like, how many people share), but there's really no focus on who those people are. You would never advertise in a magazine and say, "Oh, I got a million readers" without asking who those readers are and if it matters.

So, when you measure engagement, what really matters is whether you engaged with an audience that's relevant and that's really interested in your product. For that reason, having a large following (at least in the influencer space) is detrimental to receiving focus. So, we have to compare 2 types of influencers. For example, Kim Kardashian has an enormous audience, but it's also an extremely diverse audience. They're interested in a lot of different things and the only thing they really have in common a lot of times is that they follow Kim Kardashian. But they're not very tightly connected to her, so their decisions aren't very influenced by what she tells them to do.

Compare and contrast Kim with someone like Linus Tech Tips, who has a whole YouTube focused on tips about using gadgets. If you don't like gadgets, then you're not following him. You've probably never heard of him. But if you love gadgets, then you do follow him. You might get more engagement with Kim Kardashian as a total number, but the quality is significantly lower. Because with Linus Tech Tips, you get engagement from people who really care about gadgets and who want to see a video that explains some details; they'll be paying more attention and spending more time on those.

For that reason, I say that influencer size and traditional engagement metrics (meaning just how many people like or share) simply don't mean much.

What do micro-influencers do? There are no definitive numbers as to what qualifies someone as a micro-influencer. Yet anyone with 1,000 to about 50,000 followers can be considered as such. What separates the micro-influencer from the influencer is niche and authenticity. A micro-influencer is usually focused and passionate about their market. In continuing my conversation with Gil, I asked about micro-influencers as I believe many of the people looking to hone their personal brand can really begin to fine-tune what's important to them and why their approach to sharing it is invaluable. Here's what Gil had to say about micro-influencers:

If you think about it, everybody has influential people in their lives. When you choose which restaurant to go to, there's probably somebody you ask. When you choose which car to drive, there's probably somebody who you talk to about that – somebody that is in your circle and influential to you. And what social networks have enabled us to do is to analyze everybody that's on those networks and understand who the people at the center of a specific thing are.

What is truly unique to them is that, unlike the big celebrities or influencers, they have a very uniform audience, typically. They're experts on a subject or a niche. They have a cooking show, for example. And, by being niche, their audience becomes super uniform and, as a brand, you want to be able to target very specific audiences.

So working with micro-influencers provides you with a few advantages:

i)   *You know you're hitting a targeted audience*
ii) *Their expectations are significantly lower than the big influencers (not everybody can afford the big influencers anyways)*
iii) *It comes off as way more authentic. They're not promoting as often as the big celebrities, they're not going to promote something they don't believe in typically because their audience will immediately call them out on it, and they have a much stronger connection with their audience.*

It's easier for micro-influencers to respond to 100 comments on their posts than to 100,000 comments. So, they respond to them, they have a real relationship with them, and their audience really believes in them. And the result is that looking at them provides a significantly higher ROI. Yet I also think it's challenging because how do you find them? How do I manage to find all of the influencers in my space? I don't know all of them. That's where tools like ours help you discover and evaluate which ones are the best. But as a general rule of thumb, working with the smaller influencers always provides you with the benefits.

Brand Zones

Start today by taking advantage of the industry trade information available, even if there are fees involved. Join trade associations to network, increase your knowledge and leverage your expertise. Also bookmark or sign up for Google alerts for your subject matter or alerts from the Department of Labor, real estate trade information websites, the CDC and other applicable organizations that are relevant to your career growth path. Here is a quick checklist:

- ❏ **Set up Google alerts for applicable articles**
- ❏ **Research the top 3 organizations in your space**
- ❏ **Follow leaders on LinkedIn/Twitter**
- ❏ **Where is the conversation headed? How can you move it forward?**
- ❏ **Remain solutions focused**

The Not So Secret Change Agent

Several years ago, "change agent" became the corporate buzzword. Change agents were being hired with high-level responsibilities to turn companies around from both an internal and external perspective. These powerful people have the vision and persistence to bring out the best in individuals, processes, and strategies. They are unique in that they typically know more than others about a particular industry or system.

From a historical perspective, change agents have literally rewritten history in areas that touch our personal and professional lives. Whether it be more current figures like Elon Musk, Bill Gates, Steve Jobs, Oprah Winfrey, Mark Zuckerberg, Sheryl Sandberg, or Jeff Bezos to name a few, these individuals have chartered their own course, set their own pace for change, and winning.

Change agents are vocal. They shun the status quo. These are the leaders on the front line that are not afraid to ask tough questions, make tough decisions, and rally the masses. Some of the best change agents are able to build trustworthy relationships, which in and of itself, can create organizational and social change. How do you measure up? What areas of your industry do you see the need for change? Are there legacy systems that you see revamped? Don't just scratch the surface, dig deeper to figure out your unique value in your current career. When you do, that should be one of the primary features in communicating your brand.

When I was ready to make a career shift, people said, "What are you doing? You know nothing about branding, you know pharmaceutical. This is like the silliest thing ever!" Granted, at the time, I was not writing for *Branding Mag*, nor Forbes, nor did they see my work ethic and focus on becoming a brand leader. As I continued to operate within my core values, rehearsing my story, becoming passionate about my why, I began making noise in the branding arena. I realized that we can all become a game changer, maybe not for the world, but for our respective company, group or environment.

I completely understand and respect that everyone wants to be a changemaker or distrupter. Yes, you can take on that role in your neighborhood, in your job, or with your group. Think about where you can truly offer value and grow from there. This is a pace-setting process. Everyone wants to be next Oprah or Steve Jobs but for some reason, these aspiring agents fail to realize that Oprah and her colleagues on *Forbes Billionaires List* did not become household names overnight. Build your foundation, lay the groundwork and stabilize yourself where you are because you will inevitably encounter ebbs and flows of progress. If you are not confident and do not know who you are, people are going to tell you who you are, and you will end up on an unnecessary detour.

In an interview in *The Hollywood Reporter,* Oprah discussed why she left as a contributor to *60 Minutes*. Her response shocked me because of her renowned status around the world. "It was not the best format for me… I kept getting feedback that I was "too emotional" when recording my name. "I think I did seven takes on just my name because it was 'too emotional.' I go, 'Is the too much emotion in the Oprah part or the Winfrey part?' I was working on pulling myself down and flattening out my personality — which, for me, is actually not such a good thing." This reinforces my point. If networks wanted to redefine and tone down Oprah's essence after all of her accomplishments and lives she has changed around the globe, then we all must be absolutely confident in who we are and what we bring to the table.

RUNNER'S HIGH

No matter how you slice it, building your personal brand definitely requires you to exhibit change agent characteristics. This is where DiSC tool assessments can be of value. Your attitude, intelligence, and current role will all come into play. There is also a key accountability factor that must be included in the process. Change agents cannot succeed without a determined and persistent attitude. If you plan to remain in your industry, focus on the answers and solutions to the following questions:

1) How is your industry changing?

2) What scares you about the changes? What excites you about the shift?

3) What new skills can you acquire to make you more marketable?

4) What are you doing now to stay ahead of the curve?

When I think about my branding journey over the years I realize that all of my starts and stops were part of the process to qualify me to move to the next level. In essence, I was preparing to become a public speaker my entire career. After working for a major pharmaceutical company for several years with a great deal of personal success, I knew that I had the knowledge, skill-sets, and power to impart life-changing principles to others. As part of my preparation, I began writing articles about branding and customer experience that were picked up internationally. Not long after, I became a columnist for brandingmag.com and provided the stories and interviews on the latest brand-ing-building content available. Over time, I was invited to par-ticipate in podcasts and other corporate events with some of the leading business and brand personalities in the world. Con-tinuing that stride, lead me to tap into a perfect niche featuring corporate executives, under the C-Suite initiative which I men-tioned previously. As you continue to build your brand, you must carefully watch, study, and evolve, along with the times and consumer demand.

A= ACTUALIZE

"The story of the human race is the story
of men and women selling themselves short."
*- **Abraham Maslow***

Pace 5: 121-150 DAYS

Maintaining Your Stride

> *"Self-worth comes from one thing- thinking that you are worthy."*
> - **Wayne Dyer**

As a personally branded entity, you should be thinking about creating your value proposition so employers and other third parties will be interested in working with you. This is the time where you must find your niche to distinguish your brand from the global marketplace of potential competition. With lightning speed technology, organizations have a plethora of information at their fingertips, so your creativity in leaping ahead of the crowd should be on high alert. **YOU transcend where you work!**

In order to maintain your momentum it takes diligence, along with a passion to commit to your niche and overall purpose. How do you find your niche? Consider the things that you do better than others that don't require much effort on your part. What are those skill sets that you actually enjoy using when the opportunity arises? Partnering your work experience, educational background, and other innate skill sets will help you identify your niche in the competitive workforce. Think of your niche as the fine-tuning of the story you created in the previous chapter. All of your life experiences has molded you into the person you are today, so it is for this reason that you were destined to:

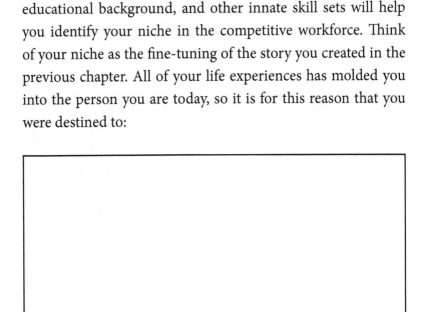

Of course, there are many others operating in your niche. However, knowing what the competition is doing is great, but don't lose focus or become discouraged. Your back story is different and you should be on what makes you different because there is room for everyone to provide their talents. Since social media hashtags are the current protocol, create your own hashtags to keep you motivated. Place them in conspicuous places to remind yourself of your goals. My hashtags are #Dream #Create # Win. What's yours?

Feeling Good

"You're so money and you don't even know it!"
- **Trent**, *Swingers*

Let's look at where you are. By now you have gone through your daily mental and physical warm-ups. You have searched inside yourself and enlisted feedback from others. You've rehearsed and rewritten your story several times. You have a better idea of how you measure up against the competition, and your research has given you good vibes about the future of your industry. I say all this because your initial preparation process should not be as painful now as it was in the beginning. You should actually feel good about your new habits and how far along you've come.

I love Trent's line above from the movie, *Swingers*. It sums up most of us; we are all good at something or better than others at performing certain tasks or being creative, yet we have challenges focusing on our gifts. Sometimes those challenges can be ourselves. I will never forget sitting in a restaurant in New York many years ago. A gentleman walked up to my table and said to me, "Can I tell you something?" "Sure," I said. "You will be amazing once you get out of your own way!" He smiled and just walked away. Turns out, this guy was a famous producer and has Michael Jackson's *Beat It* to his list of credits. I was surprised by his words, to say the least. I did not know what he meant at the time, but it certainly made sense years later. Isn't it amazing how others can see things in you that you cannot see for yourself?

Do you have a gift to sell or convince others? I remember interviewing for a job and the hiring manager asked me to sell a Number Two pencil. I felt stuck. How could I do that? Why would she ask me that? I took a deep breath, smiled, and then went into sell mode. I talked about the features of the pencil and its benefits. I believe I did well because I received an offer. I decided not to take it as I knew I could be more creative in another position. We are born with gifts, yet our gifts help make our brand more valuable.

Today, being good at something may not be enough. Author and business consultant, Jim Collins advises us to work toward being "great." You have to know your industry and find your niche. Keep in mind that your niche will grow and evolve over time, but you have to embark upon that "it" thing *now*. Commit to spending at least an hour each week to help you identify your niche by answering the questions below:

1. What are you truly good at?

The more honest and transparent you are with yourself, the better off you will be in formulating a true representation of your gifts. Don't be too hard on yourself and don't be too soft either. List these skills even if you cannot see how to monetize them at this juncture.

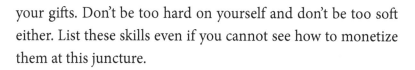

2. What skills from your list do you enjoy doing most?

I always tell people to think about what they enjoy doing the most. What makes you move inside? Do you feel something tingling in your body when you are doing it? Is there a smile on your face or in your tone when you think about it? Voilà! You have found your innate sweet spot.

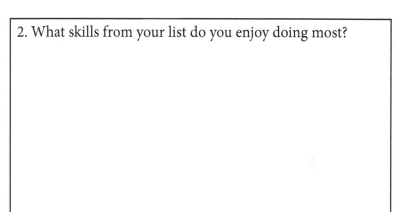

3. Do people need your product or services? Why? How?

This is where you need to begin to monetize your skills. How important are they to consumers at large? Is there a specific target audience? Do your research to see how your services stand up from an economic or public need versus want perspective. Either way, there is only one "you," so be sure to stand out.

Leading the Pack

As you are gaining the necessary brand-building momentum, what can you do to break out from the pack? What do you want to be known for at the end of the race, as well as in the future? The key to longevity is to become the walking billboard and/or spokesperson that you desire for others to remember. This requires you to align and fine-tune all facets of your brand, including your resume, business cards, and social media: LinkedIn, Twitter, Facebook, Instagram, YouTube, blogs, and website.

In order to achieve that polished and professional look, feel, and consistency, engage others to review and critique your public persona. Today, video resumes are becoming popular, so consider this as a great way to showcase your talents. Video resumes give others the ability to interact with you continuously. Each time you acquire a new skill or solve a critical problem, make a video about your accomplishment and post it to your LinkedIn or professional social media page. Practice what you want to say and post the polished video. Of course, videos will not replace face-to-face interaction, however, it will give you a significant head start over the competition. Continue to think outside of the box to stand out in a non-gimmicky manner. Focus on winning solutions to common or complex problems. Think about writing nugget-filled e-books that qualify you as an expert in your area. Post them to your videos and other social media channels.

The Sprint

As you already know by now the global competition for highly skilled professionals is fierce. Therefore, it is important to know what your service market needs and how you can help them access it. An effective technique that I utilize in most situations is to always recognize the problem, and then give my perspective on the most effective solution. Think about how can my skill sets add value to any situation? Previously, I mentioned the need for a value proposition to demonstrate what value you can add to a company or individual's daily challenges. The more knowledgeable and ahead of the curve you are for your target audience, the better your chances of maintaining your stride and getting your second wind.

a) **Brand Recognition:** Do you have a theme or brand slogan? When I was a kid I loved watching the television series *Shaft*, starring Richard Roundtree. He was a tall, dark, handsome private detective that wore all black when he was on a case. The most distinctive thing I remember about the show was the theme music. *Shaft* had the coolest theme music arranged and recorded by the late Isaac Hayes. As soon as you heard two rifts, you knew *Shaft* was about to appear on the screen. What's your theme music? Do you think you need one? How will others remember you? Have you created a to-die-for brand slogan?

b) **Accessible:** I am amazed at how many people I talk to about what they are doing to build their brand and nearly all of them speak about their social media presence. Granted, social media is important, but what are you doing to connect with actual people? Depending on your market and niche, consider small local libraries or meet-up sessions to highlight your expertise and have face-to-face conversations. Become known for being an expert who is *accessible and approachable.*

c) **Trade dress:** The golden arches, along with the yellow and red trade dress is what differentiates McDonald's from other brands. Consider the colors, symbols, as well as the emotional and aesthetically pleasing feel you want to invoke in others when they review your website or other collateral material about you. Color is important and there is a more detailed explanation of colors at the end of this chapter.

***

I was fortunate to interview Sheila Marmon, the Founder and CEO of Mirror Digital, a California-based interactive media and advertising company. Mirror Digital is targeted to multicultural markets and currently has a monthly consumer base of 25 million. Sheila's company successfully connects consumers to Fortune 500 brands daily. I asked Sheila her thoughts on professionals distributing content through various mediums to expand their personal brand. Her response was just what Coach Syd needed to hear:

"I think it is fantastic that professionals are exploiting different types of media to build their personal brands. Using a portfolio of tools builds momentum behind a message in different ways. Broadcast gives you the reach and scale to touch many people quickly while narrow-cast media, like social or local, provides a platform to develop more targeted and personal messages.

Individuals nascent to brand building can easily get started with social media because it is readily accessible and there are some compelling benefits to platforms like Facebook, Instagram and Twitter. Social media allows an individual to connect directly with his or her target audience, to facilitate one-on-one interaction, and to create feedback loops helping you better understand what your readers are seeking from you by providing metrics on engagement. "

I then asked her about the effectiveness of using social media and the pitfalls with such a platform.

"The real power of social media is that you can be as innovative, raw and unfiltered as you like. In other words, social media tools can be particularly liberating for a brand builder because there are no gatekeepers who decide what types of messages should be shared and there are no editors who judge which content is most relevant or "the best" and therefore published. But, with this power, comes great responsibility. To quote development guru Steve Covey, "Begin with the end in mind." Profes-

sionals have to remember to define their ultimate brand message and what they want to accomplish up front. Once these central questions are answered, we can dig deeper: Is the content being published consistent with the brand message? Are all media platforms relevant to your audience? If you choose to utilize several platforms, how do you determine which content resides where."

Sheila's advice is bar none. Evaluate your platforms and messages as you have just finished the race.

Brand Zones

1. Make sure all of your email addresses are professional;
2. Consider creating email addresses that identify your expertise;
3. Be creative in figuring out how you can solve a difficult problem and highlight it in a memorable way;
4. Upload professional headshot photos as well as photos of you in action speaking to a group or working with clients;
5. Have a logo created that exemplifies who you are and what you bring to the table;
6. Create a blog to engage readers to capture their emails;
7. Keep an online dialogue going with your target audience as often as possible; and
8. Feature and give credit to others who are doing things that compliment your efforts or where you intend to go in the future.

RUNNER'S HIGH

*"Skills help you get a job. Competency helps
you transcend your job roles and responsibilities."*

I worked with a client who was an accomplished strategist and finance person who helped startups go to next level. She had a multitude of skill sets in nearly every career facet. My job was to help paint a great picture but to downplay the finance industry as she was looking to transition out. The challenge in personal branding is that people get connected into an organization and their personal brand and attributes become ingrained in the organization. I advised her on the importance of her personal brand standing alone since she really was not Bank of America.

*"People remember you for what you did,
not where you worked."*

We created a skill set inventory list. I was able to narrow down three skill sets that spoke to things that truly demonstrated who she was. With the recent passing of my grandmother, I hear her voice echoing more often. She always said, "Stick with what you are good at and everything else will fall into place. No matter what you are doing, what you love and are good at, will stand out." Grandma was truly a long distance runner, who was always ahead of her time.

How To Effectively Use Color When Branding

The utilization of color can be a very powerful tool in a brand's arsenal. That said, very few brands have effectively been able to gain a competitive advantage through the use of color. On a very basic level, color has the ability to evoke emotion. On a deeper level, color is arguably the most powerful stimulus for the brain. Coupled with personal experiences, the reaction to a particular color usually correlates to where it falls on the spectrum – warmer colors such as red and yellow – are bold, uplifting and energetic. Conversely, the cooler side of the spectrum, blue and green, exude calmness and feel more reserved. This is vitally important because emotion is one of the most powerful tools to connect with consumers.

There are three key points to remember when color is being used as a primary brand differentiator:

1. It must align with your brand identity/promise
2. It must set you apart as well as work within your industry
3. It must be integrated seamlessly across the brand.

Consider these color meanings when thinking of your brand:

Black: commonly associated with power, formality, evil, darkness.

Blue: evokes feelings of calmness and spirituality as well as security and trust.

Green: symbolizes health, new beginnings, and wealth.

Orange: calls to mind feelings of excitement, enthusiasm and warmth. It is also energetic.

Purple: is the symbol of royalty, wealth, power and nobility. It is also associated with wisdom, mystery and magic.

Red: is often associated with passion and love as well as anger and danger.

Yellow: is associated with laughter, hope, and sunshine.

White: commonly associated with light, goodness, innocence, purity, perfection, and safety.

Pace 6: 151-180 DAYS

Brand Tempo Runs

"Branding demands commitment;
commitment to continual re-invention;
striking chords with people to stir their emotions;
and commitment to imagination..."
– Sir Richard Branson

I've heard the term "tempo runs" over the years and never knew what it meant. According to former Olympian and coach Jack Daniels, Ph.D. (yes that really is his name), he defines a tempo run as 20 minutes of steady running at threshold pace. If you are in great shape and an experienced runner, your pace should be around a half-marathon pace, which is pretty fast. Think of it as a fast-paced workout to build your metabolism. It is what gives you the stamina to keep going. Doing a tempo run incorrectly can ruin your training benefits. Many people misuse the term "tempo run" when they do not perform well.

Now that you are well on your way to creating your brand with five months of training under your belt, it's time to really think through your marketing strategy. Your online presence is a key requirement in today's marketplace, and the more interaction and direct feedback you are able to capture from visitors, the better insight you will have on your target audience.

There is enough information on the web regarding using and capitalizing on your social media presence so I will not reiterate information that you already have at your fingertips. Yet over the years, I've learned that social media should no longer be thought of as your single strategy. Instead, view it as another channel to advertise and market who you are. Don't forgo other marketing mediums.

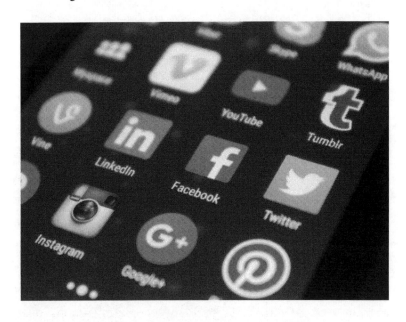

5 Golden Rules of Social Media

Be Clear
Be Authentic
Be consistent
Add Value
Engage

Online Tips

- ✱ Do all of your account profiles align?
- ✱ Take a social media audit of people you admire.
- ✱ Does your bio speak to where you are going?
- ✱ How do you close the gap in your online interactions:
- ✱ I respond to every person that views me or sends a comment
- ✱ I respond to those people that interest me
- ✱ I rarely respond to people
- ✱ LinkedIn - Always be professional and lead with experience.
- ✱ Twitter - Become a thought leader by retweeting to get on people's radar. Yes, people want to know your voice, however, follow those whom you respect. Identify 10 thought leaders in your space: Follow them, Engage, Stay engaged and Offer solutions
- ✱ Facebook - Keep it social, yet always classy. Stay away from self-promotion and providing too much personal information if you want to be taken seriously.
- ✱ Instagram - One of the best vehicles to build your brand but not without a clear strategy first. Plan your strategy: What are you saying? How are you saying it? Who are you speaking to? Be consistent.

Rules of Engagement...
If you want engagement, engage
If you want support, support

The saying, "It's not what you know, it's who you know" still holds true. There should be a section in your marketing strategy where you intentionally focus on building relationships in your respective area of expertise. Social media is great but going out and interacting with others similarly situated will provide you with additional knowledge on moving forward. There may also be opportunities to barter services or partner on a special event. Equally important is the fact that the more you know about what the competition is doing, the better prepared you can be to stay ahead of the pack.

Experienced Runners

Get insight and tips from someone who has been there before. You're never too young or old to seek out a mentor. You can learn a great deal from someone who has been there before you. A mentor is someone who has experience in a variety of areas and desires to guide and help others follow a similar path. It is important to make a list of the things you desire in a mentor and what you intend to get out of the relationship. Research those in your field who are successful and embody a few (not all) similar qualities as yourself. Send them a email and follow up with a call to see if they would be interested in establishing a mentor-mentee relationship with you. Again, keep in mind that such leaders are typically very busy, so be specific as to what you want, when you want to meet (in person or conference call), and what you hope to learn.

In addition, a mentor does not have to be someone who is more seasoned than you in their field. With ever-changing technologies and skill sets, a mentor can be someone younger than you, but they possess a skill set that you desire. This relationship can be more informal, but reciprocal as there may be something that you have to offer that your mentor needs. Always be in a continuous learning mode regardless of a person's title.

I've been fortunate to have great mentors in my life stemming from my parents and grandmother, to elementary and high school teachers, and ultimately college professors. These people always set aside time to impart knowledge or practical skills I needed. From a career perspective, working several years in the pharmaceutical industry provided me with great mentors to help hone my sales, marketing, and training skills. I was fortunate to learn from those at the height of their careers. If there is someone you really admire in your organization and desire to become your mentor, go for it. You really have nothing to lose. Chances are, they will be willing to interact with you at some point in time.

A final point on the topic of mentors and accountability partners is that in addition to having personal guidance in your corner, as a brand builder, you also need a Brand Champion. *What is a Brand Champion?* Unlike Brand Ambassadors who endorse and promote a company's product or service, Brand Champions are professionals who can help you develop and grow so that you can do business with them. It is a mutually beneficial business relationship. The more you actualize your brand, you will be able to target your Brand Champions and make the connection. **Brand Rockstars seek out Brand Champions**!

Stretch More

"A mind that is stretched by a new experience can never go back to its old dimensions."
- Oliver Wendell Holmes, Jr.

If you are currently operating within your comfort zone, you are not building your brand to its fullest potential. Take a moment to initiate a "Complementary Stretch Strategy." This means learning a new hobby or trade that can be an added benefit to your brand. For starters, since you have instant access to the world every day you can shift your thoughts to a more global mindset. What knowledge or services can you offer to organizations in China, India, or Europe? In addition, ask yourself, "What activities should I engage in or what books should I read that will provide me with a well-rounded view of my next level? Your **Complementary Stretch Strategy** should consist of:

1) Researching global experts in similar and dissimilar fields. What are they doing to stay abreast of industry and societal changes? How do they spend their free time? What makes them special to you? Your targeted global experts should become your virtual role models to spark your pace;

2) Engaging in a new physical activity;
3) Traveling abroad to get an inside look at business operations and cultures;
4) Hosting a networking event; and
5) Sharing information with other organizations.

Going Global

It is impossible to talk about brand-building without mentioning the global aspect and capabilities that need to be considered. For the past few years, several tech companies have ranked in the top ten as the most recognizable global brands. Let's face it, it's hard to imagine that people around that world never heard of Google, Amazon, Apple or Facebook. What does this name recognition trend tell us? Technology is never going away or slowing down. If anything, it says that we should continue to hone our technological knowledge and stay informed of the latest developments to not only enhance our brand but to be in line with consumer expectations. Make sure all of your links to others can be accessed via mobile devices. As a brand, you must embrace technology to engage your audience in new ways and to remain relevant.

Today's consumers are more knowledgeable and tech savvy, which means they are more influential. As your brand story builds, consumers will have a hand in adding their stories to their experiences with your brand. They are likely to feel connected and loyal to your brand which will help further your message throughout the world.

All along, I was focused on connecting with international leaders and brands. After years of my efforts, I never thought that I would host a Rebels & Rulers in Romania, speak and co-host in Cairo for Brand Summit, or help coach startups in Stockholm. But I did and there's more to come. Not to mention I was featured in an article in *Black Enterprise Magazine*, "Journey to Building a Global Brand," which is actually a dream come true as I read *Black Enterprise* throughout my youth. Take strategic steps to build your brand and get your name and talents into the global marketplace. Even if you are not a household name, your name should be well-regarded in your niche. Continue to use technology to the fullest and you will see results. My mantra is: #Dream #Create #Win.

Brand Zones

By now you should have a good idea of your target audience and brand strategy. It's been a few months of soul-searching, learning, and trying new online approaches. One of the main reasons why tempo runs work is that if you do them correctly, you get to a point where your body naturally produces lactate and hydrogen ions into your muscles. The hydrogen ions make your muscles acidic which is why you feel fatigued. However, the more tempo runs you do in your workout, your lactate threshold becomes higher because your body learns how to use the hydrogen ions better so you can run longer distances. Are you ready to run longer? You are now at the halfway mark.

The key to running and brand-building is to put in the work with the right amount of intensity. If you have pushed yourself through the exercises and questions thus far, your runner's mindset should now have a strong foundation to help you keep going. Your brand is shaping up. What level of intensity should you be at by now?

- Subscribe to and read the latest industry trade journals for your desired market for the past year to the present;

- Attended at least two conferences on your related subject matter; and

- Network, network, network! Actively network and follow up on LinkedIn. Networking is pointless without follow up.

RUNNER'S HIGH

Growing up, I wore Keds brand sneakers regularly. I never realized that it was originally a brand geared towards women. It's slogan "Ladies First Since 1916," is powerful and conveys their target market and brand longevity. Keds has reached its tempo run and created a stylish, quality brand for generations of women, men and children. There are Keds for various occasions and lifestyles, including a wedding collection, a Major League Baseball collection, a customized collection, and a fashionable line of unique colors and patterns. Keds is stronger than ever before and they are on pace to engage with their customers and meet their needs wherever they are.

I caught up with Emily Culp, the CMO of Keds. Emily works to create customer-centric experiences for women in what she calls "micro-content building." Emily stated:

"You're building micro-moments of content that exist in every single channel, but how we start building our content is we think about mobile first. Everything our consumer does is in mobile and it originates there; so we build content for mobile and then we fan out to the other channels from there. I think a second piece that's really important to me is just thinking about, again, our consumer and her lifestyle. And it is one that encompasses multiple different channels whether it's retail, online, mobile, etc., so for us, as a brand such as Keds, our job is to come up with a seamless amazing experience for her across all of those different channels."

How can you think of your personal brand in micro-moments?

C= Commit

"Accept no limits. Just do it!"
- Nike

Pace 7: 181-210 DAYS

Brand Intervals

"Progress is impossible without change, and those who cannot change their minds cannot change anything."
- ***George Bernard Shaw***

Congratulations! You're more than halfway to the finish line. You have worked hard, paced yourself, and received positive feedback as a result of your name recognition in the marketplace. Now what? You can recharge for a few days, but don't get too comfortable. This is your moment to pause and reflect. Keep the momentum going and get out there and shake hands and meet people on a larger industry-wide scale.

Brand-building requires constant action. Although registration fees for trade shows and conventions can be steep, it is a good idea to save, prepare, and plan to attend key shows for your industry or where you plan to be in the future. Not only will you be able to meet your peers, learn more tools of the trade, and sell yourself or your product or services, you will have an opportunity to make a lasting impact on others. Relationship-building will always open doors to your future.

Knowledge-Sharing

Regardless of your target market, leadership role or business acumen, paying it forward by providing information to others is a fulfilling endeavor. Why not teach a class? There are several educational outlets that welcome experienced business professionals to teach classes based on a particular subject matter. Teaching is a way to give back your personal knowledge and experiences and tap into a generations curiosity and thirst for new information.

The upside of teaching is that technology allows you to teach online classes, as well as work within a flexible schedule during the week or weekends. Usually, evening courses are designed around a professional's standard work schedule, so this will be conducive to your target market. Teaching also gives you a stage with a captive audience to engage in question and answer sessions and actually practice at public speaking, which is a critical skill set for brand-builders.

In some instances, teaching can be done on a paid as well as volunteer basis. Volunteering in your area of expertise is both rewarding and fulfilling. As a volunteer, you are receiving an insider's view of the daily challenges an organization faces. This will allow you to interact with others from various levels and make lasting connections. It also provides you with a different perspective on handling everything from policy issues, employee concerns, product or service manufacturing, distribution, customer satisfaction, budgeting and a financial overview of the organization. Whether you are a paid teacher or volunteer, being an insider within another market segment of your area of expertise is priceless.

Collateral Materials

At this stage, you should have created a great deal of content to highlight your expertise. With business and processes changing rapidly, it is a good idea to review your collateral content available to the public. You may have to revise and streamline some of your materials every six months to keep up with your industry.

Run Your Own Race ™
Half Way Mark
Brand Interval Checklist

Pace 1 - Win the Morning
- ❏ Have you started an early morning routine?
- ❏ Are you meditating?
- ❏ Journaling?
- ❏ Exercising?
- ❏ Eating a balanced breakfast?

Pace 2 - Look Inside Out
- ❏ Eliminate comparisons to others
- ❏ Remind yourself it is a solo effort to the finish line
- ❏ Trust your inner voice to propel you forward
- ❏ What three words describe you?
- ❏ What core competencies can you attach to your descriptive words?
- ❏ How can you apply your redefined skillsets?
- ❏ What makes you happy?

Pace 3 - Millennials - Gen Y
- ❏ Take time to be self-reflective.
- ❏ What is your EQ? How can you relate to others?
- ❏ Try the DiSC Assessment Tool to help you better understand yourself
- ❏ Access your skills and take steps to grow
- ❏ Have you sought 360-degree feedback
- ❏ Are there certifications that you should take to increase your marketability?
- ❏ What is your story?

Pace 4 - The Course Ahead
- ❏ How are you preparing for your industry changes?
- ❏ Are you excited about the shift?
- ❏ What are you doing to stay ahead of the curve?

Pace 5 - Maintaining Your Stride
- ❏ What do you enjoy doing the most?
- ❏ Why do people need you?
- ❏ How can you stand out with brand recognition? Theme, Slogan, Color?

Pace 6 - Brand Tempo Runs
- ❏ Research global experts in similar and dissimilar fields. What are they doing to stay abreast of industry and societal changes?
- ❏ Host a networking event
- ❏ Share information with other organizations

Brand Zones

Again, your brand interval is a time to reflect on how far you have come and to map out what more needs to be done to get to the finish line. This interval is also a time to introduce new techniques to help build your stamina. Acclaimed marathon trainer, Jeff Galloway, introduced the "run walk run," Galloway method in 1974, as a way to help inexperienced runners train their bodies to go the distance.

> *"Walk breaks will significantly speed up recovery because there is less damage to repair. The early walk breaks erase fatigue, and the later walk breaks will reduce or eliminate overuse muscle breakdown."*
> **- Jeff Galloway, Run Walk Run Method**

Galloway points out that the walk is not when you get tired, instead it should be incorporated into your entire run, as it allows your body to create endorphins for you to both mentally and physically to recover and eventually run faster and farther over time.

How can you incorporate the Galloway Method into your personal branding routine? Here are a few ideas:

- Basic: Every run is symbolic to you seeking new tools and knowledge to help you grow. Run, walk, and repeat.
- Take your time. It doesn't happen overnight. Focus on the work. Respect the process so you do not wear yourself out early and become discouraged.

- Short run vs. long run. Where is your true focus? Break up your goals.
- Get in a stride...Dedicate three days a week to your personal growth.

Brand Rockstar Tip: Brand Rockstars pace themselves throughout the process in order to endure the ebbs and flows to the finish line. Brand Rockstars must:

Embrace Fear

Execute

Add Value

Help Others

Focus on what's next

RUNNER'S HIGH

This would be a good time to volunteer with organizations that are doing positive things in your community or engaged with your target audience. Having an inside view of the inner workings of businesses can help you better position yourself in your desired area. Not only are you helping others, the relationship building and networking are priceless. Making one-on-one connections go further than having hundreds of followers with limited to no engagement. Everyone knows someone who can be helpful in some way to your brand-building process. Be positive. Be a person of your word and help in any areas as needed. Be resourceful. Your efforts will be worthwhile in the long run.

Coming Up The Rear

"Even if you fall on your face, you're
still moving forward."
- Victor Kiam

There is no time to look back. You are closing in on the others. The finish line is straight ahead. Imagine yourself riding American Pharoah or Justify. Both you and your horse have blinders on to block out your peripheral vision so its full speed ahead. All too often we get distracted from our purpose by looking to the left, right or even at our past. We begin over analyzing what we have done and how far we have come. Our progress seems minimal compared to our efforts or others. Remember, this is new territory. It's your first race. You've probably learned more about yourself by now than you knew before. Keep moving. You will persevere.

Even if you are not where you want to be in your brand-building journey, it's really OK. Accept one hundred percent ownership of what you have done thus far, what you have *not* done, and take it in stride. If you truly believe that you have a great deal to offer organizations or the masses at large, then you will finish this race at your pace, at the right time. No one can out-pace or outrun you being you, especially when you know what you want. Ask yourself, *how bad do I really want it?*

Running Solo
"You have to believe in yourself even when no one else does—that makes you a winner right there."
- Venus Williams

Often times when you set out on a path to chart your own course for personal development, it can be an emotional roller-coaster. Just know that you are not alone. Like all of us, you have that annoying self-doubt voice in your head whispering, *you're not good enough, you'll never be good enough, and you're going to fail!* No matter how you try to silence it, that voice somehow manages to creep into every goal you set or action you take to achieve it. It's not easy to just ignore it and think positive. Yet, I've realized that with authentic self-reflection, you can *learn* to eliminate self-doubt and truly believe in yourself. Belief is spiritual. It is that positive inner voice that encourages you to keep going.

Such belief should be based on facts, not fiction. For exam-ple, if you have completed your degree, certification, or train-ing in an area, then your belief that you should be counted as an expert among those in that field is valid. However, if you never take the step to attend school or train for an event, then your belief is based on fiction and you really need to work on authentic self-reflection and make changes in your daily routine. Achieving a goal or dream is something that takes deliberate effort, time and dedication. No pain, no gain.

Having a visual outcome of your belief becoming a reality is also a key step. That's why vision board parties have become popular, however, there are few metrics to determine the success rates. Many people see them more as a social gathering, rather than a results-oriented, accountability exercise. Regardless, whether you engage in vision boards in groups or create some form at home, the key is to stick to your vision. The saying goes, "if you look the part, act the part." Therefore, create a plan to begin *acting* as if you have achieved your beliefs. Whether it be in your appearance of dress, establishments you frequent, or your new routine, act as if your dream goal is about to become a reality.

At the end of the day, this is really *all* about you. Like boxing, tennis, and gymnastics, running is a solo sport. Of course, you can run on teams or play doubles in tennis or even team gymnastics, however your individual effort will be the key to your personal and team success. You get out what you put in. That is why it is so important to *Run Your Own Race*. There is no need to worry about or try to keep up with the Jones'. The competition has their own set of challenges and idiosyncrasies. They have their own training regimen. Stick to your game plan.

Brand Zones

Up until this point in your life, it should be evident by now that everything that you have accomplished is a result of your belief in yourself. That realization should be enough to propel you to continue. There is so much more that you can accomplish and it is within your reach. Tap into that higher power that is within all of us to accomplish our goals. We just need the confidence to access it. Step out and take risks. Failure is not a negative thing, its positive. You will learn from your mistakes. You will work harder. Research more and overall grow wiser and stronger.

Post these affirmations to help you continue moving forward.

Believe

Relevant

Actualize

Navigate

Dominate

RUNNER'S HIGH

Since your efforts are the determining factor in this race, always remain a person of integrity. The more authentic and transparent you are, the stronger the likelihood of connecting with your target audience. As an early personal brand-builder, you don't have the benefit of having a variety of products or services already in the marketplace so that if one product isn't working you can resort to another. Therefore, everything you do must be done with a high level or moral principles. Granted, we are human and will have a few hiccups along the way, but for each misstep, you will have to do more or give more to earn your place in the hearts of your target market.

It's commonplace these days when large corporations pay out millions and sometimes billions in class action suits for making false claims about products that in some cases cause severe injury. Whether it be car manufacturers, pharmaceutical companies, food or beverage companies, they all have ample products to bounce back into consumer trust. Remember when PepsiCo claimed that Naked was all natural and a class action suit was brought against them? PepsiCo had to refund consumers who demonstrated a proof of purchase. Refunds of $75 were given to people who had receipts and those who did not received $45. Did consumers dump Pepsi products? No, the brand is stronger, provides a diverse variety of food and beverages. Naked sales continue to soar and PepsiCo launched Naked branded fruit, nut and veggie bars. This is a smart move by the company to stay ahead of the competition and capitalize on both the snack and health food craze in today's culture. As a personal brand, you don't have the luxury of positioning several products in the marketplace, yet you have the creativity to market and bundle your skills and anticipate the needs of your audience. Learn from the successes and failures of major brands so that you can lead the pack in your field.

PACE 9 - 241 - 270 DAYS -

YOUR BRAND MARATHON

Laborious Tasks

"... my way of getting through difficult times of low confidence - hard work."
- David Beckham

This is really personal. It's where the brand-builders are separated from the brand-seekers. You're already conditioned to run a 5K or 10K with ease. You've done your homework on what it takes to build a lasting brand. Now, you must settle in and revisit everything that you have learned. Stay committed so you can continue the disciplined tasks to get to the finish line. If you give up now, you will be frustrated that you are in the same position physically, emotionally and mentally. The choice is yours. Either continue building your personal brand or make excuses about the obstacles to transformation. It is an extremely challenging feat to win a marathon the first time out of the starting gun. I don't think anyone has accomplished it. Remember, the goal is not to win, but to finish the race at your own pace. You have the tools and information, all you need now is to find that impactful defining moment.

Decision Time

It's crunch time! That defining moment in your life when you're urged to make a pivotal decision to move forward or change course. Or it occurs when you experience something that fundamentally changes you on the inside. Not only do these moments define us, but they have a transformative effect on our perceptions and behaviors.

For me, my defining moment was when I got fired from my corporate job after 10 successful years. As I mentioned earlier, it was a wake up call because I was so comfortable and would have never left the company. I tried acting and then moved into voice overs which after struggling to land a gig, I ended up voicing over 100 national brands. During that time, I stayed active on building my brand and educating myself about the industry. Without me being fired, I probably would have never continued on my brand-building journey. I recognized that comfortability breeds normalcy and I became too comfortable in my normal. Once you identify your passion, then you must embrace fear and live your purpose.

Moments that are truly defining will compel you to ask "why me?" and often challenge your beliefs to the point that you behave differently. Whether or not you lead others, think of a moment i) when your true character was revealed, ii) you had an opportunity to excel, or iii) you saw something with greater clarity. Write your responses below.

i) My true character was revealed when…

ii) I had a once in a lifetime opportunity to excel when…

iii) After all these years I finally see…

Inevitably, the road of life will be bumpy, testing your commitment to your purpose. Yet some individuals see road bumps as obstacles, while others see them as opportunities. Many people have recognized their defining moments and moved forward by:

1. **Being resilient and embracing adversity:** The irony of a defining moment is that if you don't define it, it will surely define you. View these moments as an opportunity to learn, grow, and not become stagnant. Compartmentalize the moment and quickly find purpose.

2. **Acknowledging fear:** Best-selling author and entrepreneur Tim Ferriss, said "What we fear doing most is usually what we most need to do." The beauty of a defining moment is that it usually forces us to face our fears head on and take action. I can personally attest to how scary it is, but I can also also tell you how much better you will become. Acknowledging fear helps mitigate the potential paralyzing effects.

3. **Quickly recalibrating:** Recalibrating is a function of taking an honest assessment of where you are. To move forward, we often need to know why something occurred. But sometimes, we can't identify our *why* as quickly as we would like. With stillness and meditation you may have clarity and answers. Yoga is a great way to process an event, calm the mind, and figure out what to do next. Your *why* is the foundation for building your action plan to move forward. It is essential to think beyond the defining moment and open yourself up to the innumerable lessons.

4. **Creating a (solutions-based) action plan**: Billionaire magnate, investor, engineer, and inventor Elon Musk, is known for creating action plans. From a business perspective, action plans are essential to help us benchmark progress. For me, prior to entering graduate school, I did a personal SWOT analysis to assess my skill sets and gaps. By doing this, I was able to begin my studies with the end in mind, fully aware of what was required of me to successful completion. Your plan doesn't have to be complex, but it must be specific. It's your roadmap for moving forward, and it lets you see how far you have come.

Defining moments will ultimately make or break us. According to experts, its best to identify them quickly and make the decision to positively move forward. We all have the ability to define our defining moments. Acknowledge yours and walk confidently to the starting line up.

Reaffirm Goals = Recommit

Going the distance and finishing strong is the most challenging aspect of setting and accomplishing a goal. If you're like me, in the beginning I am gung-ho to take on the new task at hand. Over time, the routine or additional work can get boring or I lose interest if I am not seeing results within the time frame I created. It's like falling off the wagon when you're on a diet and binge on junk food. What does it take to get back on track? The first thing I do is reach out to my accountability partner and confess my desire to quit. Usually, this person reminds me why I set the goal in the first place and what it means for my future if I at least try to finish.

Of course, my accountability check-person was right. Starting is great but finishing is more important as the results could open doors and unforeseen opportunities. As I have done before, I recommit to my goals and alter my schedule to switch things up. I suggest that you do the same. The idea is to get the same amount done, but maybe spread out tasks throughout the day and in different environments. For some of us, it may require recommitting each day since we may not see results whether it is increased following or feeling like you have made an impact.

Are you ready to kick things up a notch? If you are going to go the distance, then you have no choice. The competition is working overtime and consumer demand is at an all-time high. Your insight is needed to make a critical difference in your organization's bottom line. Can you deliver? If you were spending an hour a few days a week working on your audience, now you need to increase that time by at least one hour. You need to do longer runs since the finish line is within reach. As always be authentic and consistent in your revamped goals:

- *Manage* your time…set goal-pace runs into your new routine; long runs every other weekend or every three weeks

- *Manage* your intake of information; be mentally and emotionally fit
- Don't start something drastically new in routine now

Brand Zones

I believe the best part about setting goals to building your personal brand is that there is technically no time limit to end and there is always an opportunity to start over. If we view this along the theme of training for a marathon this is the time when your body is sore, the weather is lousy and you want to quit. Think about the reason you desired to challenge and push yourself to run the race in the first place. Get back to your original pace to run with ease.

Throughout this journey, we've never really focused on your training gear. As a runner, you should invest in moisture wicking fabrics and cushioned running shoes at least a half size bigger as your feet will naturally expand over time when running. As a brand-builder, determine if you not only have the right laptop or mobile phone to expand for growth yet research the best apps and other software to help maintain your brands online engagement. If you have been using various apps that are not connecting with your audience, shift gears and try at least three or four in order to analyze what is working and what's not. A rule of thumb is that any go-to app to enhance your brand must be scalable for mobile phones.

In 2019, U.S. mobile retail revenues are expected to reach $267.47 billion, up from $156.28 billion in 2017.[2] I imagine you have noticed that more people use their mobile phones to make purchases than in the past. Studies have shown that nearly half of mobile phone consumers would prefer to use their smartphones for essential purchases and other tasks. Apps can be a great asset to your brand but make sure the ones you choose are seamless and scalable to the mobile platform.

- ❑ LinkedIn
- ❑ Instagram
- ❑ Twitter
- ❑ Podcast
- ❑ Vlog
- ❑ Blog

RUNNER'S HIGH

One of the most impactful influences in my life was my grandmother. She often said, "the most powerful thing you can do in life is to make a decision." Research from Cornell University shows that adults make an astounding 35,000 decisions each day while children make 3,000.[1] Although most of these decisions are not vital, many of them determine our daily productivity.

A few years ago, I decided to pursue an MBA at the University of Miami. I was fraught with fear, mostly because I completed my bachelor's degree almost 15 years prior. However, I knew this decision would be a defining moment and have a significant effect on my life's trajectory. I also knew that if I could do this, I would show my future children and others, that anything is possible.

Two years later, my grandmother beamed as she watched me collect my well-earned graduate degree. I did it! Two years

---

1 https://go.roberts.edu/leadingedge/the-great-choices-of-strategic-leaders

following my accomplishment, she was diagnosed with lung cancer, and passed away a short time thereafter. The pain was immeasurable and the loss, irreplaceable. My grandmother's rapid demise made me a highly committed cancer advocate.

In retrospect, these two defining moments have made me a more resilient, focused and agile leader. This is largely because I knew what constituted a defining moment and how to move forward. What's your defining moment?

BEST IN CLASS BRAND

"Goals should never be easy, they should force you to work, even if they are uncomfortable at the time."
- Michael Phelps

Have you ever thought about the steps top brands take to achieve best-in-class status? Many of the same activities that corporate brands take into planning for success are similar to the steps you should take to strategize towards implementing your best-in-class personal brand. Brands like Nike, Apple, and Amazon are constantly focused on consumer experiences and engagement on a more intimate level. These brand leaders hone in on gathering knowledge of their target customer, highlighting the customer's uniqueness and passion, and are generally consistent on all marketing channels. Sound familiar? All of these key steps can also translate to assist you in becoming your own best-in-class brand.

To Thine Own Self Be True

From a personal perspective, understanding your target customer or audience relates back to your authenticity in your self-evaluation. The deeper self-knowledge of your strengths, weaknesses, and results from your DISC assessment, the sharper your focus and goals. Your main assignment is to fully understand *you*, which is your unique target audience of *one*. Go back and make sure you totally connect with your unique value proposition.

The great thing about building your personal brand is that no one can beat you at being yourself. You have already put forth your personal best, so at the end of the day in your heart, there is not much more you can do. Give yourself the OK to move on to the next goal or challenge. Since you have been working on this goal for several months, it's time to determine what separates you from those in your field touting similar expertise. To find great examples of best-in-class personal brands, you only need to look at the commitment and record-breaking statistics of professional athletes in various sports. Notably, the global success of U.S. Olympic athletes Michael Phelps and Simone Biles, who are in an elite class of goal achievers.

Although retired, Phelps is one of the most decorated Olympians of all time with 23 gold medals and 28 total. He has more medals individually than over 100 countries combined. When you think about it, Phelps worked hard in and out of the pool for 20 years. He carved out his brand in order to consecutively make the USA Men's Swim team which selects about 40 of the top male swimmers in the nation. What was it about Phelps' work ethic that differed from the thousands of other male swimmers? Did he have an advantage? Was he faced with a disadvantage? As we briefly examine his career brand, the similarities in focusing on your career-building brand will become clear.

Maintaining your commitment to succeed is a characteristic that must become part of your DNA. It is that drive which forces you to keep grinding on those days when you just don't feel like it. I recall reading an article about Phelps years ago and he stated that there were years where he swam seven days a week even on Christmas and on his birthday. Over time, he cut back to six days a week, yet still training five or six hours a day to maintain a 50 mile per week swim. Most people cannot commit to this type of routine for a number of reasons. However, what you can commit to is continuing your steady pace that has gotten you this far and being consistent.

What is it about you that stands out? Where do you see your edge over others similarly situated? For Phelps, he has more physical advantages in the pool than most people realize. At 6'4" tall, he has an arm reach three inches longer than his height to tap the wall. Not to mention that he has short legs for his height, which is another advantage in swimming. He is also double-jointed in both his knees and his feet which means they can rotate 15 degrees more than the average person, causing his feet to work like flippers. It's safe to say that Phelps was born to be a swimmer. What were you born to be? You may not have physical characteristics that give you an advantage in your field, but if you stretch beyond your comfort zone, you are bound to find that sweet spot.

One in Three Million

The true definition of unique is being the only one of its kind. How is it that brands like Apple, Nike and Louis Vuitton maintain their uniqueness? There are thousands of phone, sneaker, and handbag manufacturers around the globe. The Apple brand is known for its simplistic design and appearance. Nike is known for quality and stylish athletic footwear. Louis Vuitton is known for its quality, style and world renowned signature logo. Yet, all it takes for a brand to become unique is to find that one or more things that they do better than the competition and focus on it 24/7. Did you know that one of the reasons the Louis Vuitton bags are so expensive is that they are both waterproof and fireproof? Each handbag also goes through vigorous testing for several weeks to ensure it can carry certain weight when dropped from one foot, it is exposed to ultraviolet rays to ensure it will not fade, and the zippers are actually open and closed 5,000 times to make certain that they work. Finally, the most interesting fact about the Louis Vuitton brand is that any products not sold that year are shredded to maintain brand exclusivity. All of these superior qualities is what eliminates the thousands of other handbag manufacturers from competing.

What about you? Where does your uniqueness shine? As children, most of us were praised by our parents and teachers for our unique abilities. Yes, there is something inherently different in all of us, yet there are many things the same. From a genetic viewpoint, even though we are unique, our DNA sequence which is also called our genome variation, shows that we are all 99.9 percent the same. Yet that one percent difference literally equates to more that three million differences between your genome and someone else. Based on the aligning of the stars, those three million differences is what made Simone Biles born to be a gymnast.

At first glance, old videos of Biles as a youngster flipping all around her parent's house, there is no doubt that gymnastics would become her passion. At six years old, she was a natural. As an adult, she has won a combined total of 19 Olympic and World Championship medals, and holds the honor of being the most decorated American gymnast. In October 2018, she was set to compete the next day at the World Championships in Doha, Qatar, and was in excruciating pain. She went to the Emergency Room as her trainers thought she had appendicitis. Turns out she had a kidney stone that would not pass. Biles checked herself out of the hospital and competed in less than 24 hours and posted the highest all-around point totals for the year. She perfectly executed a difficult vault routine that is now named after her. Biles' work ethic and dedication to the sport is bar none. We all have our one and three million unique qualities that can separate us from the crowd. Fine-tune your unique selling point as your time to compete is approaching.

Love it or Leave it

There must be an inner desire propelling you to the finish line. It's called passion. The pursuit of your passion is what wakes you up early in the morning and often times keeps you up late at night. Leaders like the late Steve Jobs exuded such a genuine love and passion for Apple products that allowed him to consistently deliver greatness and create a cult-like following for every upgrade. For years, demand for new Apple products outweighed the supply. If you don't have a passion for your brand, your efforts will be minimal and your marginalized results will clearly show others that you are not serious about achieving success.

Key factors to being around for the long haul are consistency, competitiveness and exposure. As a personal brand, your audience will be loyal to you if you continuously provide the product or service that connected them to you in the first place. There will always be competition and your task will be to stay ahead of the competition and anticipate your customer's needs in advance. Do you recall when Amazon's Alexa came on the scene and everyone loved it? Google had to quickly catch up with Google Assistant. We talked earlier about who moved my mobile phone, and we have come to a point where entire households cannot function without Alexa. As a brand, it is your job to stay up to date on all of the social media platforms and other apps to grow your brand. When all is said and done, Brand Rockstars lead and innovate so their target audience remains loyal. You've made it this far, the finish line is only a few strides away. Execute!

E= EVOLVE

"Man, alone has the power to transform
His thoughts into physical reality; man, alone
Can dream and make his dreams come true."
- Napoleon Hill

THE FINISH LINE

> *"You can quit if you want and no one will care.*
> *But you will know the rest of your life."*
> **- John Collins, U.S. Navy Commander &**
> **Triathlete**

When and how you finish is all relative. This is your race and only *you can* define what it means to finish. The end goal is that you continue to evolve and add value to whatever setting you chose. Every new task that you have undertaken, every new goal completed, has prepared you for your future brand. All of us are a work in progress and the more energy we put into making progress along your journey, the higher our chances of success. It's not over. Keep making strides.

A few years ago, I studied the Kaizen model for continuous improvement. The word Kaizen actually comes from two Japanese words: Kai, meaning improvement and Zen meaning good. The English translation is continuous improvement. This model was originally intended for manufacturing industries but over time it evolved to into continuously improve all personnel functions of a business. The great thing about this process is that employees participated in suggesting ways to improve the business. I believe this thought process works well if you view yourself as a business, as your brand CEO.

Throughout this journey, we have seen that by taking small steps instead of drastic, rigorous changes, you will bring about measurable results over time.

What can you do to continuously improve now that you have come this far?

Like the iconic scene in *Forrest Gump* running through town, my advice to you is to keep running! The world is in constant motion so finishing this race prepares you for the next one… and the next one.

Brand Zones

Now that you are at the finish line, it is important to stand out from the crowd. Therefore, revisit your social media to ensure i) you have a clear vision; and ii) you have communicated your value proposition clearly. You should always be looking for ways to improve your message while staying true to your values. In addition, think about what you want to be known for. As a personal brand, you are a leader. Define what your leadership strength will be. Are you going to connect people and share information? Always remember to celebrate others in your online posts or other materials. Are you going to create new content and think out of the box often? Are you going to be an influencer? Highlight your strengths and value at all times to attract new audiences. Stay connected to your accountability partners and seek feedback from them.

The key to longevity and sustainability is to build a genuine following of engaged people. Anyone can buy followers and appear larger than life, yet being able to measure your activities will separate you from the crowd. The foundation has been laid and you have a great blueprint to work from that demonstrates you really know yourself. Go back and review the checklists throughout to ensure that you are on the right track. Continue to run and get noticed in positive ways. All of your work will pay off in ways you never imagined. #Dream #Create #Win.

Runner's High

Visualization and actualization work! All of those images in your mind of dashing over the finish line have become a reality. You now have the confidence to achieve greater things. Guess what, even if you did not finish your race within your allotted goal, it's still OK. Think about the exercises and self-evaluations that will benefit you moving forward in your career. If you've made it this far, there are more positives to take away from your experiences. Focus on what you achieved and how you can work harder to do better. Major brands look at every set back as a learning experience. What did you learn about yourself? What did you learn about others in your circle? How can you overcome the challenges from the past? Focus on solutions to running the race again and don't get bogged down with the past. The race is yours to win if you stick with the plan and take control of your future.

~

PACE 12: COOL DOWN

At the beginning of your brand-building journey, we started with the warm-up. Hopefully, you have reaped the advantages of the warm-up and set S.M.A.R.T (Specific, Measurable, Accountable, Realistic, and Timely) Goals to carry you past the finish line and into the real world of productivity and creativity. Now that you know what it takes to build a powerful personal brand, you've got to keep the momentum going. You must continue with your building routine to enhance your brand, but now it should feel more comfortable and you should see results. Even if it is only a few new engagements, continue to engage and add value.

Use this cooling down period to revisit areas where you realized more work is needed or you see another niche or shift that you can fulfill. This is your reevaluation and self-reflective period. Carefully review the answers to your questions, your story, and results from your personality tools. Everything you've done up until this point has value, so use your data wisely. When endurance athletes like marathon runners cool down, it is a necessary practice to regulate their blood flow set their body back to a normal state. Operating as a Brand Rockstar is your new normal so kick your plan into full gear!

Brand Zones

Ibelieve you should think of cooling down as your personal performance review. Most companies schedule annual performance reviews to aid in employee development. Complete your own performance review of your brand-building journey to set you on a path to growth for the next year.

Consider these cool-down activities:

- Review your "why" to ensure it still resonates;

- Revisit your value proposition; and

- Rehearse your story and tweak as necessary.

Each year you should increase your visibility, revenue, and product and service offering. This can be done by stretching outside of your routine a few times a year to learn something new to help you become more marketable. Write out short, simple affirmations to keep you motivated daily. One of the reasons most of us fall short of building their personal brand is a lack of sustained effort. It takes a lot of content and engagement for others to remember you so you must stay the course.

YOU are necessary and the world is waiting to see and hear what you have to offer. Postion yourself as a leader and become the Brand Rockstar that you were destined to be!

ABOUT THE AUTHOR

Sidney Evans is a strategist that works with companies, founders and revenue-generating startups. He is a speaker, thought leader and expert in branding and communications. He mentored young entrepreneurs in Stockholm for Start-Up

Stockholm Weekend powered by Google for entrepreneurs. He has been published and referenced in *Forbes, Branding Mag, Oracle Marketing Cloud and American Express Open forum.*

Evans is an international speaker and host, presenting his research on the most effective techniques for companies and individuals to communicate their unique story by developing clear messaging and implementing sound strategy. Most recently, he delivered his speech, "Building a Powerful Personal Brand", at the Brand Summit conference in Cairo, Egypt and he was host of the Rebels & Rulers conference for *Branding Mag* in Bucharest, Romania.

He is the creator of the "C-Suite" interview series for *Branding Mag* where as moderator he has interviewed some of the world's top C-level executives. He has been featured as one of the keynote speakers for the "Personal Branding Day" conference that was broadcasted internationally from Poland. Evans' first book on personal branding, *"Run Your Race: 12 Pace-Setting Tips to Building Brand"*, will be published June 2019. Syd received a B.S. International Business Florida A&M University and a MBA, Marketing University of Miami.

Twitter: @sydinc
https://www.linkedin.com/in/sidneyevansmba/
https://www.facebook.com/sydinc
www.sidneyevans.com

BRAND-BUILDING MEMORIES

Communicating! In the studio completing voice-over for
Chrysler Dodge Durango.

Hosting Branding Mag's Inaugural Rebel & Rulers Conference, Bucharest, Romania

Rebel & Rulers Conference, Bucharest, Romania

Mic check before speaking on Building a Powerful Personal Brand, Cairo, Egypt

For Bookings & More Information

visit <u>www.SidneyEvans.com</u>

Endnotes

1 https://www.inman.com/2019/04/19/compass-ceo-reveals-more-ambitions-to-be-real-estates-one-stop-shop/

2 Dengel, Tobias. "Four Ways to Rethink the Brand App Experience." Forbes Technology Council Community Voice. June 11, 2018. https://www.forbes.com/sites/forbestechcouncil/2018/06/11/four-ways-to-rethink-the-brand-app-experience/#577728fd5e4e

Finished!

Made in the USA
Columbia, SC
25 May 2020

98243042R10087